30 DAYS OF INSPIRATION AND HOPE

—

TROY BLACK

INSPIRE
CHRISTIAN BOOKS

www.InspireChristianBooks.com

Copyright © 2017 by Inspire Christian Books

Editor: Larissa Runyan
Supporting author & Co-editor: Reese Black
Cover photography: Troy Black

All rights reserved. No part of this book may be used or reproduced in any manner whatsoever without written permission, except in the case of brief quotations embodied in critical articles and reviews. For contact information, see www.InspireChristianBooks.com.

"Scripture quotations taken from the New American Standard Bible®, Copyright © 1960, 1962, 1963, 1968, 1971, 1972, 1973, 1975, 1977, 1995 by The Lockman Foundation Used by permission." (www.Lockman.org)

Kindling. In *Cambridge Dictionary online*. Retrieved at April 14, 2017, from the website Cambridge University Press at http://dictionary.cambridge.org/us/dictionary/english/kindling

Tolkien, J.R.R. (1994). *The Fellowship of the Ring*. New York: Houghton Mifflin Company.

Table of Contents

Day 1: A Hope That Does Not Disappoint....................06
Day 2: Kindling a Passion for the Kingdom.................12
Day 3: Hope in the Midst of the Storm.......................18
Day 4: Walking the Walk..22
Day 5: How to Have Faith in Hard Times...................28
Day 6: Dropping the Ball..32
Day 7: A Light When All Others Go Out....................38
Day 8: Living Water..42
Day 9: My Burden is Light...46
Day 10: Still and Quiet...50
Day 11: Shouldering Impossible Burdens...................54
Day 12: Authentic Forgiveness....................................58
Day 13: Bread from Heaven..64
Day 14: Extending the Grace of God.........................68
Day 15: Plugged Into the Source................................72
Day 16: Unsticking Your Lure and Your Life.............78
Day 17: Water to Wine..84
Day 18: Come Home, Child..90
Day 19: God's Wisdom and the Wisdom of Man.......96
Day 20: Cleaning House...102
Day 21: A Treasure of Great Worth..........................106
Day 22: A Key to Every Door....................................112
Day 23: A Friend for the Road..................................118
Day 24: Solving Finances God's Way........................122
Day 25: What's in a Name?..126
Day 26: Why is Being a Christian so Hard?.............130
Day 27: A Change of Clothes....................................134
Day 28: The Desire to Be a Hero..............................138
Day 29: Walking the Narrow Path............................142
Day 30: Still Believing..146

- INTRODUCTION -

I invite you to join me for the next 30 days on a journey filled with hope. As you read this book, my desire is that you will develop a closer walk with Jesus Christ and a greater understanding of His love for you. I believe that the more in step we are with our Savior, the more our days will be filled with hope and our actions will be inspired by grace.

These devotionals will cover topics such as peace, strength, direction, courage, passion, provision, and acceptance. I will use stories and illustrations to paint a clear picture of how God's amazing grace can be applied to different areas of life.

No matter what you are going through, there is a hope for your tomorrow that can only be found in the truth of God's Word and in a relationship with Him. Raise your hopes with me as we walk through the next 30 days together.

In Christ,
Troy Black

- DAY ONE -
A Hope That Does Not Disappoint

"For while we were still helpless, at the right time Christ died for the ungodly."

Romans 5:6

If there is one battle that I have fought more than any other in my Christian walk, it is the struggle with hopelessness. It is that point at which I feel as if my past has no meaning, and my future has no direction. It is that state in which I just want to close my eyes and admit that I have nothing left to give—or that what I have to give is simply not worth giving. It is not a pretty state. Hopelessness is a formidable enemy to overcome, and that is the very reason *why* the enemy tries to use it against us so often. When hopelessness begins to eat away at my joy, it is obvious what the answer is: renewed hope. When disappointment has taken over, it is time to attempt to hope again. At least, that is how we normally go about fixing ourselves, right? Time and time again, we seek to inspire, build, create, purchase, discover, or simply imagine into existence a new level of personal hope. I believe this way of thinking is the very reason we sometimes fail to find hope. No matter how resolutely we attempt to pick ourselves up on our own, true hopefulness only comes from one place. This verse from Romans reveals that place.

"Therefore, having been justified by faith, we have peace with God through our Lord Jesus Christ, through whom also we have obtained our introduction by faith into this grace in which we stand; and we exult in hope of the glory of God."

Romans 5:1-2

Romans 5 begins with a grain of hope. If you are in a hopeless position right now, this is an excellent place to start. It starts by reminding believers that because we are washed by the blood of Jesus Christ, we now have peace with God. This verse is not talking about a peaceful feeling, though peaceful feelings are nice. It is talking about a new position in relation to God. "Peace with God" means a renewed relationship with God. It means the barrier of sin and punishment, which would have kept us isolated from the presence of God for eternity, has been overcome in our lives by grace through faith in Jesus. He has made a way for us to come boldly into the throne room of God. In and of itself, that fact can ignite hope because we can know that no matter what happens here and now, we will spend eternity with a loving and gracious God.

Then, the next part of the verse takes it a step further. It says, *"we exult in hope of the glory of God."* We were created in the image of God, and the only way for us as sinful humans to rightly display His glory now is through Christ in us. What hope is Paul talking about? Because we are no longer our own, Christ lives in us. The lack of purpose we once had as sinners separated from God is replaced with a new purpose given directly through God's Son. The more we allow Jesus to change us and to make us into a new creation, the more God's purposes will be fulfilled in our lives. Not only did Christ restore our relationship with God, but He also gave us a purpose. If you are wondering what that purpose is, read Matthew 28:19-20 and Ephesians 4:1-16.

Better still, there is an even greater hope in the next verse:

"And not only this, but we also exult in our tribulations, knowing that tribulation brings about perseverance;"

Romans 5:3

The darkest tribulation that you face (the worst part of your life) can be a catalyst for constructing perseverance in you. This might not sound that great at first, but the reason it does not sound all that great is because we misunderstand perseverance. We despise tribulations. We fear hardships. What we often wish for instead is hope apart from trials. If hope is what we need, then yes, it makes the most sense to seek hope. But this is the point of our problem that I mentioned earlier: we are seeking hope in the wrong manner by trying to get as far away from the tribulations and trials as we can, and for that very reason, we are still hopeless. Look at the next verse:

"and perseverance, proven character; and proven character, hope."
Romans 5:4

Surprise: seeking or waiting for hope apart from hardship is not the answer. *Then what is the answer?* True hope enters our hearts when we respond to difficult circumstances through the workings of Jesus Christ in us. What I mean is this: Jesus understood that the terrible trials He faced were all for a greater purpose. He went so far as to willingly lay down His life on a cross. He died for a world of sinners because He knew and understood God's eternal purpose for His temporary situation. God loved us so much that He used hardship and death in Jesus' life to bring about victory for us. When we humble ourselves before God and allow Christ to live in us, He begins to steer us toward that greater purpose through perseverance. The more we persevere in Christ, the more character He is able to develop in us. The more character we develop, the more hope we have. True hope comes from a place that the flesh can never understand.

Verse five takes it one step further by reminding us of the great gift of comfort that God has given to those who are in Him:

"and hope does not disappoint, because the love of God has been poured out within our hearts through the Holy Spirit who was given to us."

Romans 5:5

God showed us His love by sending His Son to die, and He reminds us of His love by filling us with His Holy Spirit. The Holy Spirit always points back to the work of Christ, and because of this, we are able to live daily in the knowledge of God's love. It is an amazing statement that says, *"hope does not disappoint."* This does not mean you and I will never feel disappointment. It means that if you are in Christ, your hope will never die. It will always be renewed. Your hope will be rooted in a love that is so deep, it led the perfect Son of God to the cross so that He might be a sacrifice for an imperfect people. Disappointment is temporary, but the love of God is everlasting. Choose to place your hope in Jesus today.

- APPLICATION -

1. In which areas of your life do you feel hopeless? Have you given the outcome of those circumstances to the Lord?

2. Have you been trusting in Jesus for hope, or have you been seeking hope in another place? None of us are perfect, but as you persevere in Christ, you will find a hope that never ends, no matter how dark things may seem at the moment.

3. Do the other people in your life know about the hope we have in Christ as believers?

- FINAL THOUGHTS -

If you are a believer in Christ, eternity with a loving God is something that you are always able to look forward to—no matter how difficult the current trials may seem.

If you find yourself wishing that God would remind you of His love more often, I encourage you to ask Him to fill you with The Holy Spirit. He wants to comfort you and remind you of His love for you today.

– DAY TWO –

Kindling a Passion for the Kingdom

"For this reason I remind you to kindle afresh the gift of God which is in you through the laying on of my hands."

2 Timothy 1:6

Passion can come and go just like the flicker of a flame. At one point in your life, you may have had a gift that you used to impact the kingdom of God that you feel like is now no longer in operation. You may have a spiritual gift such as serving, giving, or teaching that you have not used in a long time. I believe that God has given each of us passions that He longs for us to use for His purposes, but I also believe that sometimes we can meander through life, slowly losing our passion for Him and for the work that He has called us to do. How can it be so easy to forget the wondrous glory of serving and walking alongside a loving, gentle Creator?

When I was a kid, I used to love building fires. My family would clear out a large jungle of thorny bushes, vines, and unwanted overgrowth from our yard, and then we would burn it. At other times, we would go camping and make a fire for warmth and roasting hot dogs or cooking s'mores. Because of these activities, I quickly learned some of the basics of building a good fire. My favorite part was always when we drenched it in lighter fluid, lit a match, and watched the burst of flames erupt. Though lighter fluid made it easy to get the flames going, oftentimes the fire would die out within a few seconds simply because none of the wood had caught flame. We often achieved the appearance of a great fire in just a matter of moments, when in reality, the only thing burning was the lighter fluid.

I think sometimes as Christians, we can act like event junkies. We like to host or attend Christian events that inspire passion and cause the flames in our hearts to erupt. We love conferences, Bible studies, retreats, special worship nights, and inspirational bestsellers because these are all things that ignite passion. There is nothing wrong with this, but a problem occurs when we forget that these types of things act similar to lighter fluid. What often happens is that a few weeks after the flames have had time to die down, we wonder why we no longer feel the same fire for God. We wonder what happened to the passion. Then it becomes easy to look at the great men or women of faith in our lives and become depressed because we doubt that we will ever be like them. They are like the coals of the fire that continuously burn and never go out, and we cannot even seem to keep a simple flame going in our own hearts.

When I first started building fires as a kid, my dad taught me one of the most important steps to creating a successful steady burn: you need to use kindling. Cambridge Dictionary defines *kindling* as small, dry sticks or other materials used to start a fire. The lighter fluid is great for ignition, but the kindling is essential if you want to keep that initial flame alive long enough to catch the big logs that will cause a steady burn. What some of us need in our walk with Jesus is not more jolts of ignition. We need to begin to take the small sticks of God's Word each day and meditate on them in our hearts. We need to begin transforming our hearts into easily combustible material by spending time in God's presence, praying, and seeking His face. If we ever want to get around to becoming coals for the kingdom of God, we need more day-to-day kindling. If you want to know how current great men and women of faith got to be the way they are, ask them about their daily habits. Ask them how often they pray.

If that stirs a feeling of discouragement in your heart, then let me refresh you. How much you pray is not the main issue. How often you read the Word of God is not the main issue either. You may be thinking, "Is this true?" Yes, the main factor affecting our passion for God is our love for Him based on His love for us. Whether we have passion for the kingdom or not depends on whether we are in love with our Savior or not. If you lack passion, start by asking God to remind you of His love for you. When you fall in love with Jesus, the prayer, worship, and study of His Word will come naturally. Remember, God's love for you is not based on your performance. Our efforts should not be based on duty, but instead on His intense, perfect love. Once we accept His love in our hearts, we will automatically begin stacking kindling on the fire out of a desire to be closer to Him.

God has given every one of His children gifts to use for His kingdom purposes. If it has been a while since you have experienced the passion that comes with doing the work of the Lord, and if the only time you ever feel the stirrings of your gift is when you are at a special worship event, then it is time that you start putting a little kindling on the fire. It is very easy to let church attendance turn into a weekly douse of lighter fluid, but God never intended for our passion to live off of lighter fluid. He wants to set the fire ablaze in your heart today, but for this to happen, you have to first be reminded of and accept the unending love He has for you.

1 Thessalonians 5:16-18 says,

"Rejoice always; pray without ceasing; in everything give thanks; for this is God's will for you in Christ Jesus."

God wants us to continuously pray because He wants us to be on a more intimate level with Him. He wants our relationship with Him to grow, and He knows that happens when we spend time with Him. As we continue to accept His love through faith, we are drawn deeper into friendship with Him. As the intimacy grows, the passion ignites, and then the kingdom impact occurs.

- APPLICATION -

1. What gifts has God given you to help you complete your calling as a believer in Christ? Have you asked Him to reveal those gifts to you?

2. Have you been giving thanks in all things? What areas—even circumstances that you dislike—could you begin to thank and praise God in?

3. Are you attempting to rejoice because of your situation, or are you wholeheartedly rejoicing in Christ? When our joy comes from Him, it never runs out.

– FINAL THOUGHTS –

When you became a child of God, you received a purpose. You have a calling that is irrevocable, and a daily habit of seeking the Lord, praying, praising, and reading the Word of God can stir your heart's desire for His kingdom work. However, remember to allow His love for you (not a sense of duty) be the motivating factor behind your pursuit of Him.

If you feel like you have let God down in this area, then let me remind you that His love does not rest on your works. Christ Jesus already finished His work on the cross, and there is abundant grace and compassion for a new beginning with Him. Now is the best time to start.

– DAY THREE –
Hope in the Midst of the Storm

"The cords of death encompassed me, And the torrents of ungodliness terrified me... In my distress I called upon the Lord, And cried to my God for help; He heard my voice out of His temple, And my cry for help before Him came into His ears."

Psalms 18:4, 6

When I was a child, I loved rainy, stormy days. The lightning would crash out of the clouds and then disappear once more, leaving behind nothing but darkness and a myriad of raindrops. I would hear the pounding of water on the roof and the sloshing of streams in the yard. Despite all of this, I liked stormy days mostly for one reason: I hardly ever got wet. While it was pouring down outside, I was dry inside. My siblings and I would often construct pillow forts to hide out in while the storm passed. I found reassurance in that no matter how terrible the weather got, we would all be snuggled up, eating snacks and simply waiting.

Sometimes in life we get hit with storms, and it can easily feel like they appear out of nowhere. I remember a storm I faced one time that I thought was going to overtake me. This was a time in my life when I battled fierce loneliness and depression, and I felt like I had done everything I could to get out of it. Despite my efforts, it looked like God was going to let me drown in the rising waters. I was afraid that He had forgotten about me, but one day He reached through my disbelief and despair and reminded me of who He was.

Proverbs 18:10 says,

"The name of the Lord is a strong tower; The righteous runs into it and is safe."

In the middle of my despair, He brought this verse to my memory, and I responded the way I often had as a small child: I got out of the rain. I ran to my Lord. When I first started to seek Him, the storm that I was facing did not immediately disperse. Instead, I found refuge in my God; I found hope in the midst of the storm.

If you feel like you are lost in the darkness of life's storms—you feel the rain pounding on your face, making it difficult to find a way through—do not be discouraged. Seek Him, and He will be your refuge; He will be your strong tower. One of the best places to start seeking Him is in His Word.

David says in Psalm 27:14,

"Wait for the Lord; Be strong and let your heart take courage; Yes, wait for the Lord."

During this particular storm in which I found myself, I wanted God to simply stop the rain, but God wanted something better for me. His desire was for me to find shelter in Him and to wait for Him even during the hardship. Earlier in the same passage, David reminds us of the promise that God makes to those who take refuge in Him.

Verse 5 says,

"For in the day of trouble He will conceal me in His tabernacle; In the secret place of His tent He will hide me; He will lift me up on a rock."

When you are hiding in His presence, it does not matter what is going on around you. He gives you perfect security, which allows you to have perfect hope. If you feel as if you are not in a good enough place spiritually to run to God, remember that He has already paved the way for you with the blood of His Son, Jesus. We can come confidently into His presence simply because of His amazing grace, and we accept that grace through belief in Him as our Savior and Redeemer. Our access to His friendship is based on His love for us, not our efforts for Him. When we draw near to Him in faith, He is our refuge and strength.

In Psalm 31:19-20a, David says,

"How great is Your goodness, Which You have stored up for those who fear You, Which you have wrought for those who take refuge in You, Before the sons of men! You hide them in the secret place of Your presence from the conspiracies of man."

Finally, verse 24 leaves us with this comfort:

"Be strong and let your heart take courage, All you who hope in the Lord."

- APPLICATION -

1. Has your situation caused you to lose hope? There is a hope that circumstances can never steal away, and that hope is found in a deep-rooted faith in Christ and His love for you.

2. Are you spending more time seeking God or wishing that the storms would just pass? Have you asked God what He may be saying to you in the storm?

- FINAL THOUGHTS -

My encouragement to you is to spend time with Him. Get to know Him on a more personal level, and allow His love and His Spirit to renew your strength.

– DAY FOUR –

Walking the Walk

> "Therefore, my beloved brethren, be steadfast, immovable, always abounding in the work of the Lord, knowing that your toil is not in vain in the Lord."
>
> 1 Corinthians 15:58

Living the Christian life can become stale when nothing good seems to be coming from our efforts for the Lord. When I put all my energy toward making an impact for His kingdom, and then it comes up short, I just want to give up. If you find yourself in that position now, then let me encourage you to take another look at the motivation behind your walk. I believe that to truly experience the life-altering blessings of God, our hearts must first be filled with the life-altering love of God. If you are working out of duty and not love, then I want to remind you that the way we receive His love is through belief. It takes us hearing the Word of

God and believing it. When His love becomes our motivation, His Spirit uses us as effective vessels for His kingdom. I want to show you an example of someone who believed the words that God spoke.

Abner is a somewhat overlooked yet very influential person in the Bible. Abner is the military commander of the army of Israel during the reign of King Saul's son, Ish-bosheth. At this time, David has been made king of Judah, but he is not yet the king over Israel. While Israel and Judah are at war with each other, Abner steps up and does something that no one else has the courage to do.

In 2 Samuel 3:9, Abner says,

"May God do so to Abner, and more also, if as the Lord has sworn to David, I do not accomplish this for him."

To fully understand this statement, you must realize that Abner is the commander of Israel's army, the army that is currently fighting David. Abner (even though he is on the side that opposes David) believes that God has made David a promise—that David would be king over all of Israel. When Abner makes this statement, he is basically saying, *I will see to it that David gets to be king like God said.* This means that he believes the word God has spoken.

Yet somehow, Abner retains his position as commander of Israel's army. While the current king,

Ish-bosheth, leaves Abner alone out of fear, Abner begins to make some important calls:

> *"Now Abner had consultation with the elders of Israel, saying, 'In times past you were seeking for David to be king over you. Now then, do it! For the Lord has spoken of David, saying, "By the hand of My servant David I will save My people Israel from the hand of the Philistines and from the hand of all their enemies."'"*
>
> 2 Samuel 3:17-18

There is a well-known phrase that goes, "don't talk the talk if you can't walk the walk." I know this phrase is overused, but it is also true. However, I want you to look at this phrase differently than you may have before. God does not desire for us to walk the walk in our own efforts. He longs to fill you with His love, and through the Holy Spirit He wants to empower you to keep walking in faith. Abner knew what it meant to "walk the walk," and his ability to carry on against heavy odds was based on the fact that he believed the words of God. While everyone else was simply talking about God's plan for David to be king over Israel, Abner stood up and took the necessary steps to make sure that it came about.

Proverbs 14:23 says,

> *"In all labor there is profit, But mere talk leads only to poverty."*

The people of Israel had landed themselves in a place of spiritual poverty, and because of this, they were not experiencing the blessings that God had planned for them. Abner had heard others talk about God's plan, but one day he made the decision to believe the word and act on it. Because of his work, David was made king over Israel, and the nation was then able to receive the benefits of living under a godly leader. We get to experience God's blessings in our lives by believing the Word He has given us too. The best place to start is by believing in the work that God has already accomplished on our behalf:

"But God demonstrates His own love toward us, in that while we were yet sinners, Christ died for us."
Romans 5:8

If you feel burnt out from working hard without seeing results, then it is time to rest in the grace of God. We are able to work only because of Jesus' finished work on the cross. Impact happens when our work is motivated by grace (provided by God's love), and we accept that grace in our lives through belief in Him. When we are resting in His love, He begins to work through us to create lasting results.

Israel witnessed the blessings of kingdom work because of Abner and because of their new king, David. If you have simply talked about God's kingdom or listened to others talk about it, then it is time to stand up and take a hold of the plan that God has for your life. It is time to do the kingdom work that God has given you to do. Thank God that the real work He requires from us is simply to believe:

"This is the work of God, that you believe in Him whom He has sent."

John 6:29b

When we believe the words He has spoken, He fills us with His love and begins to work on us from the inside out. The work that He accomplishes in us today is all based on the work He has already accomplished on the cross. If you will begin to walk in belief, you will see the profit that follows the labor.

- APPLICATION -

1. What is one thing you could start doing to affect others for Christ?

2. What is something that may be getting in the way of what God has called you to do?

3. Do you get discouraged if you do not see an immediate effect while doing God's work? Remember that one of the main blessings of working for the Lord is getting to do things with a loving Father through His strength.

Even if you do not see immediate change in others, your relationship with God will grow as you begin to partner with Him through faith. Thankfully, it is not up to us to accomplish the work. It is up to Him, and He has promised to complete the good work He has started.

- FINAL THOUGHTS -

Never doubt the importance of the work God has for you. Many Christians believe that they are not doing important things in God's kingdom because they are not a full time pastor, preacher, or missionary. Preachers are needed, but what is needed even more are God-honoring Christians in their own circles of business, politics, families, and friends. Ask God to show you what work He specifically wants to accomplish through His love at work in your life.

– DAY FIVE –

How to Have Faith in Hard Times

"For You have rescued my soul from death, My eyes from tears, My feet from stumbling. I shall walk before the Lord In the land of the living."

Psalms 116:8-9

Hebrews chapter 11 is often referred to as the "Hall of Faith" because in it, the writer briefly relates the stories of several faith-filled people from the Old Testament. Though we may desire to have an impenetrable faith like Noah, Abraham, Sarah, Joseph, or Gideon, sometimes it feels impossible to have faith in hard times. I would like to go through three key points from Romans and Hebrews that show how to have faith during times of difficulty. I also believe these truths are vital to living a life of faith on a day-to-day basis.

The first point is to read the Word of God in response to His love. When we choose to not just study the Scripture out of duty, but instead to really pursue Him through His words because we want to be close to Him, our faith is renewed.

Romans 10:17 says,

"So faith comes from hearing, and hearing by the word of Christ."

Jesus speaks the truest words that any man can ever say because He is the Truth. He gave us the tools for living a life filled with faith, and those tools are recorded in the gospels. A responsibility rests on us to respond in belief to the truth that is written. Every time you read the words of Jesus under a banner of grace, God's Spirit will show you something new—something life-changing. Though the gospels are incredible, Jesus has not just spoken the words in red. Because Jesus is and has always been God, every word that is inspired by God comes from Jesus Christ. This means that each part of God's Word is filled with His Spirit, His life, and His faith-building power. You want to know how to have faith in hard times? Read about His love for you in His Word, and then believe it.

The second point is to remember where it is you are headed. When hard times are getting us down, it can be easy to only focus on the here-and-now. However, God has another place prepared for us, and it is important for us not to lose sight of it. Going back to the "Hall of Faith" chapter in Hebrews, the writer shows us that those who lived by faith did not merely concentrate on their current location, but through belief in the words of Jesus, they had another place in mind.

Hebrews 11:15-16b says,

"And indeed if they had been thinking of that country from which they went out, they would have had opportunity to return. But as it is, they desire a better country, that is, a heavenly one."

God has created a better country for us! He has built a better city where there is no sorrow, pain, lack, or hardship. We can trust God to prepare a good place for us in eternity because of the immense love He has shown us through the work of Jesus on earth.

This leads me to the final point: we can have faith in hard times by focusing on what God has done for us through Jesus Christ.

In Hebrews 12:2, Jesus is called *"the author and perfecter of faith."* Then verse 3 says, *"For consider Him who has endured such hostility by sinners against Himself, so that you will not grow weary and lose heart."*

Jesus went through the most difficult hardship when He laid down everything for you and me and allowed Himself to be crucified on a cross. He knows what you are going through, He hears your every word, and He loves you so much that He has fully paid the price for you to receive salvation through faith. If He has loved us this much, then how can we not expect Him to see us through our current circumstances? God has already given you a measure of faith. He knows what you are dealing with and He knows what you need. If you are wondering how to have faith in hard times, seek Him and He will hear you. He is, after all, *"the author and perfecter of faith."*

- APPLICATION -

1. Can you identify an area of your life that it is hard to trust God in? Do you have a testimony of a specific time when God came through for you?

2. Would you say your attitude is affected more by the promises in God's Word or by your circumstances?

- FINAL THOUGHTS -

Faith in God requires trust in His person and character. We can get discouraged if we have believed something for a long time without results. Faith is not believing really hard that a specific dream will happen; faith is trusting God that He truly does love us—that He has good things in mind for us.

- DAY SIX -
Dropping the Ball

"For the Lord God helps Me, Therefore, I am not disgraced; Therefore, I have set My face like flint, And I know that I will not be ashamed."

Isaiah 50:7

During one summer, I went on a trip to the beach with my wife and some of her family. One day, while I was wading out into the water, I suddenly realized that I was still wearing my wedding ring. Now normally this might be fine, except that my fingers are oddly shaped and my wedding ring likes to come off sometimes while I am being active. As I was walking out into the water, I suddenly realized the danger of taking my ring out into the big waves. Fortunately, my wife happened to be standing nearby, so I decided to give her my ring to wear under hers to prevent it from being dropped or lost in the water. It seemed like a good plan, but as I pulled the ring from my finger and began to hold it out to her, I was struck with a small wave, and the ring fell from my hands and into the ocean. I quickly reached down and caught it between two fingers, thinking I was out of the rough. As I got a hold of it, another wave swooped by, and my wedding ring slipped through my fingers and away from my sight.

My heart sank the moment I realized that it was gone. My wife was standing only a few feet away, and I had just lost the physical symbol of our commitment and love I received on our wedding day. A strong sense of failure rushed over me. I felt like I had let her down through carelessness and lack of forethought. I did not want to tell her, but I knew I had to. As I broke the news, my head filled with all the things I should have done to prevent losing the ring. I thought that if I had only done things a little differently, then I would not have lost the item of value that she had entrusted to me.

Oftentimes, we do the same thing with our failures in life. We have all messed up—we have all lost hold of something that God has entrusted to us. Each one of us has dropped the ball at some point, or in this case, the wedding ring. We often take precautions and make an effort to do things the right way, hoping to successfully navigate the path that God has given us to walk. Through carelessness or foolishness, it can feel like we still let God down. He entrusts us with a calling, marriage, friendship, son or daughter, or choice, and we wind up dropping the ball. We do not mean to, but it happens anyway. Then we look back and wish that somehow we could make it all better, or start over and do things a little differently. We think that by reasoning out what has happened, we can justify our actions or rectify them. No matter how many times we go over it in our heads, the wedding ring is still gone.

I was reminded of something important the day I lost my wedding ring. My wife reminded me that she does not love me because I never mess up. She does not love me because I am perfect, and her love for me is not tied to a piece of jewelry. She loves me because she made a covenant with me on our wedding day, and no matter how many rings I lose, she is still going to love me. God is not waiting for us to drop the ball so that He can remind us of our failures. He is waiting for us to turn back to Him and lay our failures at His feet so that He can remind us of His love for us. If you feel like you have let God down, lay your mistakes at the feet of Jesus. When you seek Him, you can hear His voice saying, *I made a covenant with you.* His covenant was sealed through the blood of Christ that was shed on the cross.

God sent Jesus to die for our sins before you or I ever made one mistake. God even already knew the very sins we would commit when He decided to pay the price for those sins. It is encouraging to know that our mistakes have all been washed away, and we get to live in freedom when we accept the perfect love that God has offered us through faith in His Son Jesus.

Psalm 118:1 says,

"Give thanks to the Lord, for He is good; For His lovingkindness is everlasting."

This verse reminds us of two things. First, God's love for us is unending. Second, God is good. This means that no matter how many times we feel like we have dropped the ball, God never drops the ball. No matter how many times we feel unlovable, God still loves us. Run to Him. Lay any failures or sins at His feet, and let Him remind you of His love for you.

- APPLICATION -

1. Do you ever feel like you are carrying around a heavy burden of personal guilt or shame? Remember, God does not want believers to be full of negative feelings. Christ came to bring you life and to put you in right standing before God. If you have accepted Christ's work on the cross, you are blameless in His eyes.

2. Is there someone in your life whom you feel like you can never please, or someone in your past who was quick to point out your mistakes and failures? Forgiveness is an important step in fully receiving God's love. When we ask Christ to help us forgive the people who made us feel like failures, the barriers in our hearts begin to come down and we start to walk in an even greater freedom.

3. How do you think God the Father views you as His child? If you are a believer, I promise that because you now have the righteousness of Christ, He is not disappointed in you.

– FINAL THOUGHTS –

Sometimes as Christians we think we are supposed to walk around feeling guilty because the Holy Spirit convicts us of sin. However, the Holy Spirit points out our sin because He loves us. He wants to be closer to us, and He hates to see us do something that will cause hurt to ourselves or others.

Conviction should lead us to quick repentance so God can give us power over sin and fill us with His love again. Conviction is very different from a longstanding guilt or shame, which tries to separate us from God by making us feel undeserving of His love. God does not see you as a failure, and He does not want you to see yourself as a failure. You are an overcomer in Christ.

- DAY SEVEN -
A Light When All Others Go Out

"This is the message we have heard from Him and announce to you, that God is Light, and in Him there is no darkness at all....but if we walk in the Light as He Himself is in the Light, we have fellowship with one another, and the blood of Jesus His Son cleanses us from all sin."

1 John 1:5, 7

If you are following Christ, more than likely, there will be times when you feel like you have reached the end of your rope. It could be that you feel that way right now. You might be sitting there reading this, thinking that you have had to bear disappointment one too many times, or that life has finally gotten the best of you, or that you have just had enough. The Christian life is never a perfect life because we are not living in a perfect world. When you step out your door in the morning, you are stepping into a world full of darkness. In some cases, the darkness you face may even be in your own home. No matter what you may be up against right now, God has provided a hope for you that will never let you down.

In my opinion, one of the grandest stories ever written is *The Lord of the Rings* by J.R.R. Tolkien. In the first book of the trilogy, *The Fellowship of the Ring*, Tolkien writes about a Hobbit named Frodo who embarks on an incredibly difficult and perilous journey to destroy the one ring. During this quest, he faces many dark trials. In this book, Frodo and his company meet an elf queen named Galadriel, who gives Frodo a wonderful gift to aid him on his journey. She beautifully says, "May it be a light to you in dark places, when all other lights go out."

You may or may not be a *Lord of the Rings* fan, but it is not hard to see the usefulness of a light that never goes out. When Frodo finds himself lost in dark caves and being hunted by a monster, he remembers the light that was given to him. When all other hope is lost, the light that he carries shines into the darkness, and makes a way for him to pass.

As children of the King, we have a light that will never go out. No matter how black the night seems at the moment, the gift that God has given us in His Son, Jesus, will continue to shine into the darkness, making a way for us to walk.

John 1:3-5 says,

"All things came into being through Him, and apart from Him nothing came into being that has come into being. In Him was life, and the life was the Light of men. The Light shines in the darkness, and the darkness did not comprehend it."

Jesus is the believer's source of light. When you choose to follow Him, it does not matter what perils may arise. He will continue to shine when all the other lights go out. He will continue to lift you up when everything else in your life lets you down.

Verse 9 of John 1 says about Jesus,

"There was the true Light which, coming into the world, enlightens every man."

Have you remembered Him in the dark? Have you sought Him when you have felt lost? If you will seek Him with your whole heart today, I promise that He will shine not only into your life, but He will also make you a light to those around you. When His love fills your heart, you will not be able to help passing the gift of His light on to others.

Proverbs 4:18 says,

"But the path of the righteous is like the light of dawn, That shines brighter and brighter until the full day."

If you feel like this verse does not apply to you, remember that your righteousness is not based on works. Our righteousness as believers is based on the finished work of Jesus, and when we believe in His work, His light shines in us to light our path.

- APPLICATION -

1. Do you feel like you are just surviving the Christian life rather than thriving? It is easy to become passive and try to wait out life's difficulties. Instead, I encourage you to lay your struggles at His feet and allow Him to fill you with His love through the work of the Holy Spirit in your heart.

2. Do you see yourself as a light to others? What would showing others the light of Christ look like?

- FINAL THOUGHTS -

Christians can experience burnout after long periods of dealing with difficult people or trying to care for others. Oftentimes we place too much responsibility on ourselves to change others. At other times, we get in the habit of always giving and never being refilled. Remember that it is Christ who lives through us that allows us to be a light to others. We must take the time to let Him in so that He can shine through us. Our love is limited, but the love of Jesus never runs out.

- DAY EIGHT -
Living Water

"As the deer pants for the water brooks, So my soul pants for You, O God. My soul thirsts for God, for the living God; When shall I come and appear before God?"

Psalms 42:1-2

One of the reasons I am saddened to see summer end is that I love visiting the beach. Beaches have a lot of sand, sun, and water—a combination that spells *fun*. But no matter how much water there may be at the beach, water is one thing that you ironically should never forget to bring along during a beach trip. Ocean water, though plentiful, is undrinkable in its natural state. Have you ever been knocked flat by an incoming wave and received a mouthful of salt water? It is an unpleasant experience. The taste is dreadful. It can have a negative effect on your health, and can make you vomit if you drink too much.

In order to quench your thirst when you visit the beach, it is important to bring bottled water. Now, bottled water is unlike ocean water because it has been purified. It is not full of salt and other nasty ingredients. Ocean water will dehydrate you, whereas bottled water will keep you hydrated.

Drinking ocean water reminds me of something that many of us are too familiar with. When you consider the draws of life—the things that look inviting—there really is a big ocean of temptations out there to swallow. The world will offer you so many ways to satisfy your thirst, and at first they will look good. I am talking about the love of riches. I am even talking about happiness. Believe it or not, I am also talking about friends, family, food, and fun. The ocean is anything that we can convince ourselves will satisfy us. Now, several of the things I have listed are not intrinsically bad. The problem comes when we try to fully satisfy our thirst with these things instead of with the love of Jesus. Other things may satisfy for a while, but in the end, they will leave you with salt in your mouth. Depending on how many worldly attractions you swallow, you may even vomit them back up.

The good news is that there remains one source that will never fail to satisfy. Similar to how bottled water has been purified and made ready for drinking, the living water that Jesus Christ offers us is pure. It is complete, reinvigorating, fully hydrating, and truly satisfying. On top of that, when we experience life in a spiritually hydrated state, we are then able to fully enjoy the good things God has provided.

John 4:13-14 says,

"Jesus answered and said to her, 'Everyone who drinks of this water will thirst again; but whoever drinks of the water that I will give him shall never thirst; but the water that I will give him will become in him a well of water springing up to eternal life."

In this passage, Jesus is talking to a Samaritan woman at a well. The living water that He refers to is Himself. He desires for us to be filled with the Holy Spirit and to become truly alive in Him. It is easy to look around at the waves of opportunity that lap up around us and begin to believe we will somehow be satisfied by things that were never meant to satisfy on their own. We were created with a need for our Creator, and because of our sin we also have a need for a Savior. Jesus died on the cross so that through His sacrifice, we would have access to living water, and by drinking it, we will never be thirsty again.

If you feel thirsty today, and life is just not satisfying you, it is time to seek the One who never fails to satisfy. Trust in the finished work that He has completed on the cross. Praise Him for it. Sit and talk with Him, and allow Him to remind you how much He really loves you. He will give you the strength to live for Him, and His love and mercies will never fall short of your need.

- APPLICATION -

1. From what do you gain your day-to-day satisfaction? Do you find yourself searching for satisfaction in work, leisure, or people? Is your hunger for God greater than your hunger for the attractions of life?

2. When you pray, do you do so mainly to ask God for favors or to grow closer to Him?

3. Do you believe that Jesus can satisfy all of your needs?

- FINAL THOUGHTS -

It is easy to feel guilty about not spending enough time with God. We think that if we were better Christians, we would read our Bibles more, go to church more, or get up earlier to pray. However, if our focus is wrong, we can turn what is supposed to be a relationship into a series of religious acts to make ourselves feel holy. God does not want you to spend time with Him because it is what "good Christians" are supposed to do. He wants to spend time with you because He loves you. Learn to invite Him into everything you do during the day. Let His love satisfy you. Religion cannot satisfy—only Jesus can.

– DAY NINE –
My Burden is Light

"I have been crucified with Christ; and it is no longer I who live, but Christ lives in me; and the life which I now live in the flesh I live by faith in the Son of God, who loved me and gave Himself up for me."

Galatians 2:20

Perhaps you have heard the story of the tortoise and the hare. Well, I would like to tell you the story with a few updates of my own.

One day a tortoise was challenged to a race by the fastest rabbit in the meadow, and the first to reach the other side of the glen would be the victor. The tortoise knew that he had no chance of winning because of his slow speed. He had given up in his mind before the race even started. Just before the race, an older, wiser tortoise approached the young racer turtle. "How are you're chances?" he asked. "Not good," the young turtle replied. "I'm too slow to possibly beat that rabbit." "Well if you want to win the race, then I know something that will help," said the wise tortoise. The wise tortoise left and soon returned holding a huge kite. "I found this in the forest," he said. "When you start to run, carry it with you and you will win the race." The young tortoise looked at the elder like he had gone nuts. "If I have no chance of winning while just carrying myself, then how will carrying something else help me?" he asked. "Just trust me," said the old turtle.

The young tortoise decided to carry the kite. They lined up, and as the gun sounded, they both took off. The rabbit went speeding away as quick as can be, leaving the young turtle in the dust. But as the turtle walked, he noticed something. The kite that had at first appeared to be a burden now grew lighter and lighter. As he picked up speed, he could feel his feet just beginning to lift off the ground. Before he knew it, he was no longer carrying the kite, but now the kite was carrying him. To everyone's amazement, he came soaring across the finish line in first place.

Is it possible that we Christians sometimes see the words of Jesus as a heavy burden?

Jesus said in Matthew 16:24b,

"If anyone wishes to come after Me, he must deny himself, and take up his cross and follow Me."

This statement can sound almost scary to those of us who are overburdened or feel like we have too much responsibility in our lives already. This thought naturally arises from a real human need for time, energy, and provision. It is easy to think that if we spend too much time doing the work of God, then perhaps we will not have enough time to take care of our own needs. However, the truth of this matter is encouraging when we look at it with a correct perspective.

Jesus said in Matthew 11:29-30,

"Take My yoke upon you and learn from Me, for I am gentle and humble in heart, and you will find rest for your souls."

Jesus defies fleshly logic and tells us that His burden will give us genuine rest. It may not make a lot of sense in our minds that a greater burden equals greater rest, but Jesus said it—not me. True rest can only be found in Him, and in allowing Him to work through us toward what He has called us to do.

Mark 16:15 gives us a clear picture of what our calling looks like as we follow Christ. It says,

"And He said to them, 'Go into all the world and preach the gospel to all creation.'"

When we accept the spiritual truth that the calling of Jesus is a restful one, we are then able to fulfill that calling by sharing God's love with others. Learn to let go of the distracting worries of life. God knows what will bring you the most peace and joy. Take His yoke upon you today, for in Him is true rest.

- APPLICATION -

1. Have you ever viewed God's calling on your life as a restful one? Do you know what gifts God has given you to help you fulfill your calling?

2. Is it easy for you to talk to others about Jesus? Why do you think it can be difficult sometimes? One way to start is to simply tell someone about something good that God has done in your life.

- FINAL THOUGHTS -

We can often feel pressured to share the gospel with more people. Although encouragement is helpful, it is important to realize that we will never be very effective at doing something we dread. For example, if street ministry is something that makes you extremely uncomfortable, it is not likely that you will talk to random strangers about Jesus very often. You will have greater impact in an area if you have a God-given passion for it. God specifically designed you to build His kingdom in a unique way. Begin to ask Him what that looks like for you, and ask for a passion for that work.

- DAY TEN -
Still and Quiet

"Because you are sons, God has sent forth the Spirit of His Son into our hearts, crying, "Abba! Father!" Therefore you are no longer a slave, but a son; and if a son, then an heir through God."

Galatians 4:6-7

I remember one night when my daughter, Mirabelle, was a small baby. I began to read her a children's book. Perhaps I should more specifically say that I *attempted* to read her a children's book. She squirmed so much that she barely even looked at the characters on the pages. As she rolled around and crawled back and forth, I kept picking her up and placing her back in front of the book. Reading a book was the first part of the routine we went through every night before bed. The next step would be to sing her a short song. Finally, we would pray and then lay her down for the night.

Sometimes the routine seemed impossible to get through. This particular evening when she was being especially uncooperative, I found myself saying to her, "If you'll just sit still and be quiet, we will get through this a whole lot faster." As I said these words to my child, I saw a picture of myself and God.

I am under the impression that one of the reasons God designed childhood to last so many years is because children help teach us lessons that take most of us a long time to learn. When we accept Jesus Christ as our Savior, we enter into a family of believers. Guess which role we get to play! We are God's children, and God is our Father. Why is it that God chose to use the structure of the family as a picture of His relationship with His people? The answer should be simple to see: we often act a whole lot like whiny, loud, squirmy children who do not realize that their point of view is less than the best.

It can be difficult for us to believe that what we can see and understand with our natural eyes is not all there is. In fact, we sometimes struggle to believe that our Father knows what is best for us. Even so, the truth is that a loving parent can always understand more, see further into the future, and be able to make better decisions than a baby.

As children grow older, they still have to listen to their parents. They also begin to understand that waiting patiently, and sitting still and quiet, are actually beneficial responses to what their parents say.

Isaiah 30:15 says,

"For thus the Lord GOD, the Holy One of Israel, has said, 'In repentance and rest you will be saved, In quietness and trust is your strength.' But you were not willing."

In this verse, God speaks to the children of Israel, reminding them that their attitude should have been one of repentance, rest, quietness, and trust. Instead of taking on this attitude, they had chosen to react negatively to His instruction.

The same way loving parents desire good for their child, God desires good for His children. I understand that earthly parents make mistakes, but God's love is perfect. When we act like the unwilling children of Israel, I believe that it is because we are not accepting just how much God really does love us. We may not want to listen to God's wisdom, we may not desire to seek Him, or we may even make mistakes that we feel like we cannot bring to Him. Through all of this, God still loves us perfectly.

God still wants us to draw near to Him with our mouths *and* with our hearts (see Matthew 15:8). In order to do so, we need to accept the childlikeness that precedes repentance and trust. We need to rest in Him instead of relying on temporary comfort. God loves you more than an earthly parent could ever love you, and He really does know and desire what is best for you.

How He demonstrated His amazing love for us is stated best in 1 John 4:9. It says,

"By this the love of God was manifested in us, that God has sent His only begotten Son into the world so that we might live through Him."

– APPLICATION –

1. Do you believe God really desires your best? What does the Bible say about God's plans for you?

2. Can you identify anything in your life that goes against the will of God? Will you trust God's love enough today to ask Him to help you overcome in that area?

– FINAL THOUGHTS –

Not everything that happens to you is God's will for your life. There is an enemy against us, and people's poor choices can also have detrimental consequences. Our fallen world contains tragedy, and this can often create distrust toward God. Some people always see tragedy as punishment from God, but thank God our punishment was taken by Jesus on the cross. Even in hardship, God can be trusted. God is a good Father, and He does not want us to suffer needlessly. He wants to give good gifts to His children, and when we surrender to Him completely, His good plan is made active in our lives.

- DAY ELEVEN -
Shouldering Impossible Burdens

"Yet those who wait for the Lord will gain new strength; They will mount up with wings like eagles, They will run and not get tired, They will walk and not become weary."

Isaiah 40:31

In high school, I took a wonderfully educational yearbook class. During the first semester of the year, I was required to do a few photography projects. My favorite project included going out and staging trick photos. Trick photography can be so easily managed nowadays with the help of digital editing tools, but it used to require a lot more creativity when snapping the actual photo.

I loved the one method of trick photography where someone places their hand directly below a large object, making it look from the camera angle as if they were holding up an incredibly heavy mass.

You can find all sorts of examples online of people "holding up" things like the Eiffel Tower, the Statue of Liberty, Wills Tower (formerly Sears Tower), and other famous monuments and structures.

Although this trick is fun to photograph, an individual would be delusional if they believed that what they did in the photo was possible in real life. If the person in the picture began to imagine that they really were that strong—that they could actually lift something as heavy as the Eiffel tower—they would have a serious predicament on their hands, and an even greater problem if they attempted to do it.

When we carry burdens in life, and I am talking about the heaviest of burdens, it can be tempting to think that we possess the ability to do it alone. There are many books, movies, and songs out there that tell you that if you dig deep enough inside yourself, you can do anything. The truth is, we will never be able to live up to the pictures of ourselves these voices are painting in our minds. Now, I am certainly not telling you to never try, and I am not telling you to live without courage or determination. I am saying that God never meant for impossible burdens to be placed on *your* shoulders.

Mark 10:27 says,

"Looking at them, Jesus said, 'With people it is impossible, but not with God; for all things are possible with God.'"

It is easy to understand that, no matter how hard someone tries, one cannot lift the Eiffel Tower alone. It is impossible. Why then, do we allow ourselves to believe that we can shoulder the heavy burdens in life without the aid of the Creator? Anyone who tells you that you can do all things apart from Christ is a liar, no matter how well meaning they may be. God did not intend for you to have to bear your burdens alone. He intended—and has already made provision for—His Son to bear your burdens for you.

Isaiah 53:4a says about Jesus,

"Surely our griefs He Himself bore, And our sorrows He carried."

Jesus took even the greatest burden that we have ever faced when He took our sins from us on the cross. We see this written in a similar verse:

"and He Himself bore our sins in His body on the cross, so that we might die to sin and live to righteousness."

1 Peter 2:24

The reason Jesus bore our burdens is simply because God loves us, and He knew that we could not pay our debt off alone. Instead of acting like the weight is not hurting you, I encourage you to stop what you are doing and lay your cares upon Jesus.

- APPLICATION -

1. What is the heaviest burden in your life at this time? Do you feel like you are shouldering most of the weight?

2. Can you think of any times God lifted a burden off of you or helped you carry one?

3. Why do you think Jesus was willing to carry our burdens for us? I believe that it is because He and the Father are one. Jesus loves you enough to give everything in exchange for you. He showed that love on the cross.

- FINAL THOUGHTS -

Rather than simply asking God repeatedly to take a burden from you, it may be more helpful for you to allot time in your day to sit in God's presence. One good way to enter into His presence is through worship. As you wait upon God, He will strengthen you.

God has not promised to completely erase every burden from our lives, but He has promised to live through us. When Jesus is living in us through the work of the Holy Spirit, our burdens get transferred to His shoulders. We need to take the time to be built up by Him, or we will be lacking strength as we attempt to walk in our own ability. He never meant for us to bear our burdens on our own. Wait for Him, and allow Him to carry the burdens He has already promised to bear.

– DAY TWELVE –
Authentic Forgiveness

"To the Lord our God belong compassion and forgiveness, for we have rebelled against Him."

Daniel 9:9

Some of us are walking around with a list of people in our heads that we are holding something against. At the worst, we are waiting for the opportunity for a blatant revenge. At the best, we are simply trying to avoid thinking about those who have hurt us. If either of these instances are true, the problem we are dealing with is unforgiveness. The bad news is that unforgiveness steals our freedom. The good news is that we can experience renewed freedom in our lives when we forgive others the way that God tells us to forgive. Even when we do not feel like it, we have the ability to forgive because of God's amazing love at work in our hearts through the Holy Spirit. The Bible is full of situations in which hurt people were able to forgive with God's help, and I want to talk about one instance.

The story of Joseph is an unusual one. A lot of modern stories that involve someone being unmistakably mistreated end with him or her being avenged in some way. The story of Joseph is different because though he receives the opportunity to take vengeance, he makes the decision to forgive a crime that had life-long effects on him.

If you are familiar with the story, you know that Joseph's jealous brothers sold him into slavery in Egypt. Because of God's providence, Joseph eventually became the top man over the country only under Pharaoh. Though Joseph went through slavery, prison, and the threat of death because of his brothers' wrongdoings, he one day arrived at a place of blessing. Even though Joseph would have been sorrowful due to the loss of his family and home, it is easy to imagine him eventually getting over his misfortune and embracing his new life. Because of the blessing he experienced, some may guess that it was not hard for him to accept his brothers back into his life when they came riding into town years later. However, there is a problem with thinking that Joseph chose to ignore his feelings of unforgiveness simply because he had made it big in life. The truth is found near the end of the story, before Joseph's brothers even realize that it is he to whom they speak.

Genesis 42:24 begins by saying,

"He turned away from them and wept."

This occurs directly after Joseph's brothers admit to their sin in causing harm to their brother at a young age. Now, why is this verse so important? It is crucial because it is not often that you weep for someone you have not forgiven. It is clear that Joseph recognizes his brothers' repentance, and it causes him to be emotionally overcome. Later in the story, Joseph weeps again over his younger brother who never harmed him. At this moment though, he weeps over seeing a group of siblings that messed his life up.

In Matthew 18:35, Jesus says,

"My heavenly Father will also do the same to you, if each of you does not forgive his brother from your heart."

In this verse, Jesus is talking about the judgment of God, and His meaning is very clear: God expects us to forgive others because He has forgiven us. Oftentimes, we try to substitute real forgiveness with something counterfeit. However, the key to forgiving is found in the same passage. Jesus uses a parable to tell us that we should have mercy because He had mercy on us. God paid for the opportunity to forgive us through the life of His own Son, Jesus. Everything you have ever done was placed on Jesus on the cross, and yet He offers you forgiveness when you accept His sacrifice and simply ask for it in faith. Our power to forgive comes from His power of forgiveness working in us.

Deciding not to get even with someone is not forgiving them. "Getting over" what someone did to you is not forgiving them. Real forgiveness comes from the heart—a heart that is changed by the love of Jesus.

Keep in mind, it is not always going to be an immediate thing. Sometimes forgiveness is a process. Joseph probably did not decide to forgive his brothers the very moment he saw them. More likely, God had already been preparing and working on his heart over the years. Then, when they finally arrived, he was once again able to see them as the brothers he loved.

God did not just decide to accept us suddenly either. Jesus first had to go through a world of hell in order to make a way for us to receive forgiveness when we hear and accept the gospel. God did not just get over what we did, and He did not decide to simply treat us with kindness despite our sin. He cast the sin completely from us, and because of this, we can receive His complete forgiveness. We need to do the same for others.

- APPLICATION -

1. Can you think of anyone that, if something bad happened to him or her, it would make you happy to see? Is it possible that you are holding onto unforgiveness toward them? I encourage you to ask God to fill your heart with love for that person through the Holy Spirit.

2. Do you ever feel like forgiving someone is unfair because the person never received any consequences for their actions? Remember, the consequences for all of our sin is eternal death and separation from God. Jesus' death on the cross was completely unfair because He took our punishment, and we had nothing to give Him in return. Have you asked God to help you forgive like He does?

- FINAL THOUGHTS -

One reason unforgiveness is so dangerous is because its presence creates a weak point in your life for the enemy to attack. Unforgiveness can go three ways: unforgiveness can be toward others, directed at yourself, or held toward God. People do not always think about those last two. There may be something you did in your life that God has forgiven you for, but perhaps you have yet to forgive yourself. If you have trusted God to forgive you, it is time to also forgive yourself.

There may also be something you have blamed God for, whether you have realized it or not, and you may still need to release any associated bitterness at His feet. He is perfect, so He never needs to be forgiven. However, we are not perfect in our performance, so we still need to choose to let go of things that we have held against Him. Do not bury unforgiveness and try to forget about it. Ask God to show it to you, and let Him help you to forgive through His love in your heart.

– DAY THIRTEEN –
Bread from Heaven

"Look at the birds of the air, that they do not sow, nor reap nor gather into barns, and yet your heavenly Father feeds them. Are you not worth much more than they?"

Matthew 6:26

It often seems that, when we lack provision, we quickly forget what God has already done for us. It should make sense that if God said He would provide, and He has provided for us in the past, He will continue to do so. However, our logic tells us that what we can see is all there is. When we choose to believe this, we forget that Jesus Himself told us that He is the Way. He *has* made a way, and He *will* make a way. As in the case of the Israelites, the desert of lack that we walk through is often only as big as our complaints.

In Exodus chapter 16, the people of Israel grumbled against Moses because they were hungry.

They could see no evidence of provision, and so the people complained of their hunger to their leader. What they failed to realize though, was that their complaints were really aimed at God their provider instead of Moses their leader.

Verse 8 says,

"Moses said, 'This will happen when the Lord gives you meat to eat in the evening, and bread to the full in the morning; for the Lord hears your grumblings which you grumble against Him. And what are we? Your grumblings are not against us but against the Lord.'"

When provision looks scarce, it is easy to become bent out of shape about it for others to see and hear. Have you ever complained about lacking something to your friends, spouse, boss, or family? You may not have realized that the Lord is also a recipient of your words. If you are wondering why complaining to others counts as complaining to God, let me remind you of an important promise in God's Word about provision.

Philippians 4:19 says,

"And my God shall supply all your needs according to His riches in glory in Christ Jesus."

God promises in His Word to be our supplier. He promises to provide for those who are His. When we complain that there is not enough, we complain against the very one who has made Himself responsible; we complain against the Provider.

Why, then, does God allow us to feel a lack of provision? Though it may seem this way, God is not slacking off when our needs are not met. Look at what God says a few verses earlier in Exodus.

Chapter 16, verse 4 says,

"Then the Lord said to Moses, 'Behold I will rain bread from heaven for you; and the people shall go out and gather a day's portion every day, that I may test them, whether or not they will walk in my instruction.'"

God already has a plan for how He is going to provide, but He also waits to see how His people are going to react to His promises. He has promised to be our provider, but oftentimes we take on the responsibility of provider when we choose to doubt what God has said about money in His Word. Are you walking in faith with your finances? When we choose to believe God's Word, He takes the responsibility of providing for us into His hands.

If you have found yourself complaining about lacking something, God is full of lovingkindness and forgiveness. Remember that He has already made a way, and He really does want the best for you today. In fact, He has loved us so much that He met our greatest need: salvation through His Son, Jesus Christ.

Jesus said in John 14:6,

"I am the way, and the truth, and the life; no one comes to the Father but through Me."

If God has provided us with such a great gift, will He not also meet our other needs? *Trust* Him. He knows how to rain bread from heaven.

– APPLICATION –

1. How often do you find yourself complaining about not having enough of something?

2. Are you responding in faith to the money principles found in God's Word?

3. Do you remember God's promises when you have a need?

– FINAL THOUGHTS –

As we believe in God to provide for our needs, one question to ask ourselves is this: "What am I doing with what God has already given me?" When we are faithful and generous with the time, energy, and money God has allowed us to have, then He blesses us with more. Jesus says to seek first the kingdom of God, and He will provide the rest. God wants His blessings toward us to grow His kingdom.

– DAY FOURTEEN –
Extending the Grace of God

"For if you love those who love you, what reward do you have? Do not even the tax collectors do the same? If you greet only your brothers, what more are you doing than others? Do not even the Gentiles do the same?"

Matthew 5:46-47

When I was a young boy, a man knocked on my parents' door asking to use the telephone. He had been walking a long while through the pouring rain, and he had already been rejected by a few people after asking to use their phone. My mother invited him in to use our phone, and he left soon after finishing his call. As he went strolling down the road once more in the rain, my mother quickly mixed up a cup of hot cocoa and took it to the man along with something to keep the rain off. At the time, I remember being confused as to why my mother would go through so much trouble for some guy she had already helped. It was not until many years later that I learned how important it is to look out for the interests of others and not just our own. Because He loves everyone, not just believers, God has called us to extend the amazing grace He has shown us to our fellow man.

It certainly is easier to love people that we have nothing against, but it is more difficult when we are called to love people that really get under our skin. Have you ever thought that someone got what they deserved when a tragedy struck? Even as Christians, we can be tempted to allow ourselves to view others in this way. We must remember that Jesus looked at people differently. He allowed people who hated Him to mock, beat, and kill Him, and yet He forgave them as they were engaged in these very actions. When we were born again, we got away free, unscathed, because of His sacrifice for us. Should we refuse our fellow man the love Jesus gave us?

Before he was king, David was being unjustly pursued by King Saul. Saul was jealous of David and wanted to eliminate him because he threatened his right to rule. At one point, David got the chance to kill Saul and free himself from his perilous flight, but He took the opportunity to do something that probably shocked the men who were with him. David snuck up on Saul while he and all his men were asleep, and yet David did not even touch him—though it may have appeared that he would be justified in doing so.

Afterwards, David gave Saul a reason for his actions in 1 Samuel 26:24,

"Now behold, as your life was highly valued in my sight this day, so may my life be highly valued in the sight of the Lord, and may He deliver me from all distress."

David knew that God had anointed him to rule, and in a sense, Saul was standing in his way of accomplishing what God had called him to do. He could have easily used this as an excuse for taking Saul out, but instead he valued Saul's life, similar to the way Jesus values ours—the same way He valued the life of that man walking in the rain.

Philippians 2:4 says,

"Do nothing from selfishness or empty conceit, but with humility of mind regard one another as more important than yourselves; do not merely look out for your own personal interests, but also for the interests of others."

Sometimes it is easy to be selfless for the sake of other believers, but God's love extends beyond His children. God calls us to love one another, even those who have not accepted Jesus as Lord—even those who express hate toward Christians.

When we look at those around us to whom we have the opportunity to grant mercy, do we remember the mercy that has been shown to us? Were we not all at one point living in disobedience and on a road to destruction? I believe the key to loving others is to remain firmly rooted in the love of Jesus. No matter how bad off we were, and no matter how bad off we may be at this moment, Jesus showed us compassion because of His love for us. We get to be witnesses of the grace and love of God when we extend that grace and love to others.

- APPLICATION -

1. Are you remaining in the love of Christ?

2. Is there anyone you avoid or wish would get out of your life because they are difficult? I encourage you to ask God to help you view them through the lens of His love.

- FINAL THOUGHTS -

Our default behavior is to treat others the way they treat us. If someone is mean to us, we are mean to them. If someone yells at us, we yell at them. The world expects us to act this way, and that is why difficult and inconvenient people are actually our biggest ministry opportunities. Our love toward these types of people demonstrates Christ to the world. The next time someone difficult shows up in your life, consider him or her a God-given chance to administer His love to the world.

– DAY FIFTEEN –
Plugged Into the Source

"Can a virgin forget her ornaments, Or a bride her attire? Yet My people have forgotten Me Days without number."

Jeremiah 2:32

One day when I was hungry, I got out a piece of bread, placed it in my toaster oven, twisted the little timer dial, and waited for my toast to be ready. When I opened the toaster oven several minutes later, I noticed that my attempt at making toast had failed. The bread that I had put into the oven came out in the same condition that it had been at the start. After examining the toaster oven, I realized that there was something vitally wrong with my operation of the machine: it was not plugged in! The oven was not attached to a source of power, and therefore it had no ability to change my bread into toast.

Our Christian walk can be very similar to my attempt at making toast. Have you ever dealt with an issue so difficult to solve that, no matter how hard you worked at it, you just could not seem to fix it? When I tried to cook bread, I set the timer and waited. However, no matter how well that timer worked, nothing productive happened. I waited and waited, only to end up no closer to having my need met.

No matter who you are, at one point or another, you will face issues in life. Maybe you are having trouble paying the bills, or maybe your children are acting up and you cannot seem to handle it anymore. Your issue could be as common as finding purpose or direction in life. No matter what you may be facing right now, we all have areas in which we wish we could see some change.

I want to remind you about a group of people that faced a dire need—an issue they had no ability to change on their own.

When I read the book of Judges, the actions of the Israelites often remind me of needy children. God gives them the Promised Land, flowing with milk and honey, and yet they still disobey Him and wander away from His good plan. Because of their choices, they even find themselves wrapped up in bondage to another people. This captivity is a big issue—one that they are not able to fix. However, when they cry out to God, He sends them a man named Gideon to lead them to freedom.

Now, Gideon is certainly not the Israelites' first choice for a leader. He has zero credentials, but God chooses him to lead the people to freedom nonetheless. The key to God's plan is that He is going to be the one doing the work. Gideon is simply a vessel. Like my toaster oven, Gideon has no ability to make a change without being plugged into the source.

In Judges 6:14, God says to Gideon,

"Go in this your strength and deliver Israel from the hand of Midian."

However, Gideon replies in the next verse,

"How shall I deliver Israel? Behold, my family is the least in Manasseh, and I am the youngest in my father's house."

Gideon makes a fair argument, but God still has bigger plans.

He says in verse 16,

"Surely I will be with you."

Gideon knows that he is not cut out for the job. Israel has a serious problem in this passage. The people of Midian have oppressed them severely and they have little hope of making a change. Just like Israel, you may feel like there is little hope for change in your life right now. You may feel like your need is too great, that you have worked too hard, and that you have run out of options, but let me show you what happens when you start to daily connect with God on a deeper level.

Verse 34 says,

"So the Spirit of the Lord came upon Gideon; and he blew a trumpet, and the Abiezrites were called together to follow him."

Gideon suddenly becomes a leader, but not on his own. He gets plugged into the Source—the Lord God. When he chooses to believe the words of God, his belief leads him to obedience. God fills him with power, and he leads the entire nation of Israel to victory. The least likely candidate makes a lasting change because he is filled with the Spirit of God.

If you have worked as hard as you can with no luck, then the key may be to stop working. God has not called you to do it on your own—in fact it is impossible for you to do it alone. You can try as hard as you want, and you can wait as long as you want, but the timer ticking down does no good on its own. It is only when you get plugged into the Source that you can expect to have the power to change your circumstances. When you get plugged into God, He makes the change through you, and it is almost as if you are just tagging along for the ride.

Growing in your relationship with God starts by believing His Word and waiting on Him. When the need arises, if you are in close relationship with your Creator, you can hear the Holy Spirit saying the same thing He said to Gideon: *"Surely I will be with you."* Go to Him. Seek His presence. Listen to His Spirit. Then stand back and witness the change.

- APPLICATION -

1. Is there a need in your life that has not been answered yet? Remember, "waiting on the Lord" does not mean to simply wait for God to do something. It means spending intentional time with Him. You can believe that He will strengthen you as you rest in His presence (based on Isaiah 40:31).

2. How often do you go to God and wait for Him to speak to you? Do have an agenda of what you want to say and accomplish every time you pray, or do you allow God to set the theme of your discussion?

3. Are you trusting in the gift of grace that Jesus has won for us on the cross or in your own ability to make a change in your situation? When Jesus purchased your righteousness, He purchased your right to be called a child of God. God wants to give good gifts to His children. It is up to us to believe His Word, wait upon Him, and ask in faith.

– FINAL THOUGHTS –

You have an incredible call on your life. That call includes being used by God to change people's lives for eternity. However, the first step in completing our calling is to respond to the Father's invitation to be His son or daughter—to be continually known and loved by Him. Jesus told us that without Him we can do nothing (see John 15:5). We need to remember to be loved and strengthened by His Spirit as we seek to fulfill the calling we have as believers.

– DAY SIXTEEN –
Unsticking Your Lure and Your Life

"How blessed is the man who does not walk in the counsel of the wicked, Nor stand in the path of sinners, Nor sit in the seat of scoffers! But his delight is in the law of the Lord, And in His law he meditates day and night."

Psalm 1:1-2

One Sunday afternoon, I strolled down to the river to do some fishing. I had been casting for a while with no luck, so I decided to find another spot along the bank. I reared back and gave the pole a quick spin and let the lure fly. Unfortunately, it landed square in the middle of a patch of weeds growing next to the bank upstream. I began to reel in the line and suddenly received a harsh yank, notifying me that I was indeed stuck in the brush. Being the intelligent fisher that I am, I began to yank back, pulling right and left, this way and that, to unstick my hook.

It took a good deal of pulling, but finally it came undone and shot up into the air, flying past where I was standing and landing in another patch of weeds along the bank downstream. I again decided that the best method to secure its release would be to yank once more on the line. I hiked my pole up in the air and shook it as hard as I could, and finally the hook came loose once more and shot through the air toward where I was standing. Right when I thought I was in the clear, my line wrapped itself up into the tree I was standing under, catching the hook on an overhanging branch. It had turned into one of those days when you wished you had stayed home. I started to yank on the pole once more, but this time I had no luck. I was beginning to feel stuck.

As I stood there on the bank, unable to fish because my hook never landed in the right place, I realized that my predicament resembled life. Sometimes life can make us feel stuck. We can get so caught up and tangled in an impossible situation that we are unable to accomplish what we were meant to be doing. The more we yank on the line, attempting to free ourselves, the harder that hook digs into the situation and reminds us of how stuck we are. Now, I am not just talking about the consequences of sin. I am talking about any time when life heads a direction that we do not expect, and we feel like we are powerless to get back on course. Know today that, no matter how stuck you may feel, God desires for you to be set free.

As I stood there looking at the line, wondering why my attempts at getting it unstuck were so unsuccessful, I realized that I was working on the wrong end of the line. The sticky situation had nothing to do with my rod. It had everything to do with the hook. If I was going to make any progress in fixing the situation, I had to go to the source of the problem. With this in mind, I began to pull on the branches of the tree until the hook came all the way down into reach, and I was able to gently untangle the line and detach the hook from the tree. When we are facing a sticky situation in life, we sometimes pull as hard as we can and fail to make any progress. The truth is that God has placed the keys to releasing the source of the problem in His Word.

Have finances got you stuck? Look at what God says in His Word:

"Give, and it will be given to you."

Luke 6:38

Stop worrying about how much you have coming in and start looking at how much you have going out. The problem might be on the other end of the line. Now, I know this issue takes courage, but I encourage you to look at it from a relational perspective, and not a dutiful perspective. God wants the very best for your finances because you are His child and He loves you.

Has your health got you stuck? Look at this verse in Romans:

"But if the Spirit of Him who raised Jesus from the dead dwells in you, He who raised Christ Jesus from the dead will also give life to your mortal bodies through His Spirit who dwells in you."

Romans 8:11

The answer may not be to only seek the cure, but rather to also seek the Healer. God cares about your body—He really does. How many people did Jesus turn away who asked Him for healing? Matthew 15:30 tells us that He healed those who came to Him. The Holy Spirit has the same heart for healing that Jesus did.

Has worry got you stuck? The apostle Paul says:

"Be anxious for nothing, but in everything by prayer and supplication with thanksgiving let your requests be made known to God. And the peace of God, which surpasses all comprehension, will guard your hearts and your minds in Christ Jesus."

Philippians 4:6-7

Perhaps it is time to stop seeking peace and start seeking the Provider of peace. The answer to every sticky situation is not in the situation itself. The answer is in our relationship with Jesus Christ.

No matter how bad off things may seem to us, God never gets stuck. When you have tried to free yourself and you are out of energy, give the outcome to God. Go to His Word. He wants to be your everything. He demonstrated the boundlessness of His love when He made the greatest sacrifice in order to save us. God gave His own, innocent Son over to murderers on our behalf. We could not get unstuck from sin ourselves, and Jesus would rather endure pain and death than see us in bondage. He willingly endured it, and that is why we get to live in freedom today. God loves you enough to die for you. Believe that He loves you enough to free you from your current struggle.

- APPLICATION -

1. When you have a seemingly impossible problem, how often do you go to God's Word for the solution? God's Word is not a list of rules. We know this because it even says that the rules were not able to save us (Romans 8:3). Instead, it is a love letter from a Creator to His creation. The Bible tells us how a loving God did the saving through His Son Jesus.

2. Is it easy for you to ask God for help, or do you feel like you are bothering Him? Remember, God saved us so that we could be with Him for eternity. God wants to spend a lot of time with us, so we never have to feel like we are bothering Him when we pray.

- FINAL THOUGHTS -

When we feel stuck in life, we often go to others for advice. Counsel is definitely a good choice, but I would encourage you to seek Godly counsel when you are in trouble. The difference is whether counsel directs you to solutions that are based in the truth of God's Word or not. It is a good sign if they bring up examples of how God helped them in similar situations or how they found an answer in the Bible. If not, you may simply be getting instructed on how to struggle in your own strength. I also encourage you to find believing friends who you can grow with as you walk through life.

– DAY SEVENTEEN –
Water to Wine

> "...walk in a manner worthy of the calling with which you have been called, with all humility and gentleness, with patience, showing tolerance for one another in love, being diligent to preserve the unity of the Spirit in the bond of peace."
>
> Ephesians 4:1b-3

God has a calling for your life. If no one has ever told you before, let me be the first. God has a calling designed specifically for you—meant to fully utilize the gifts, talents, and passions that God has given you. If you have heard this and yet have never seen evidence of such a calling, then I encourage you to examine the underlying motivation of your walk with God. If you feel like God forgot to give you a calling, look back to the cross Jesus shouldered for you. Jesus loved you so much that He carried His own cross to die on, so that you could be forgiven and made free when you believe in Him. The same God who understands your need for salvation (and loves you enough to do something about it) also understands your need for purpose. He understands and has a calling for *you*.

In the second chapter of John, Jesus performs the very first miracle of His ministry years on earth. Jesus and His disciples are attending a wedding feast and the wine has been depleted. After Jesus' mother asks Him to do something about it, she instructs the servants to do whatever He tells them.

Jesus says in verse 7,

"Fill the waterpots with water."

As humans, we are designed to function with ambition. We have plans, goals and desires that we long to complete. God also has good plans for our lives, and when we begin listening to Him, He may tell us to do something that does not fit within our plans. He may tell us to start using our time to fill waterpots. What I mean is, He may tell us to do something that does not make a whole lot of sense. We may have a hard time understanding how God's leading fits within our God-given calling. During these times, it is important to remember that God knew us from the beginning. He designed us and He is the one who has called us. He is the one who has called you.

Jesus' request probably seems odd to the servants. They could take the opportunity to complain, saying, "People have already washed. Why are we filling waterpots? This is not bringing us any closer to getting more wine for the guests. It is not moving us any nearer to our goal. It is not helping us fulfill our purpose." However, after they do fill the pots with water, Jesus tells the servants to take the water to the headwaiter for tasting. When the headwaiter puts the glass to his lips, he is no longer drinking water, but instead, it has changed into the best wine he has ever tasted.

Verse 9 says that the headwaiter

"did not know where it came from (but the servants who had drawn the water knew)."

Because the servants listen to Jesus, they get to witness a miracle—the first miracle of His earthly ministry. What a privilege!

We may feel like what God has currently asked us to do is worth no more than buckets of water, but God has a greater plan in mind. The world will tell you that your time is only worth what you put into it. Some people will say that what you are doing for God is a waste of time (someone may have said the same thing to the servants at the wedding). God had a greater calling in mind then, and He has a greater one in mind for you now. If you will learn to take Him at His Word and remain faithful in the task He has given you to do, God will transform the little things into much. He will transform what others thought was worthless into something of great value.

God has a calling for each and every one of us, and the first step to discovering and fulfilling that purpose is allowing Him to root us firmly in His love. I know I have been talking about obedience, but we are not even capable of being obedient apart from Him.

Jesus says it this way in John 15:5:

"I am the vine, you are the branches; he who abides in Me and I in him, he bears much fruit, for apart from Me you can do nothing."

When we draw near to Him in belief, resting fully on the finished work of Jesus, He fills us with the Holy Spirit and then empowers us to listen and obey what He is saying. God does not expect our obedience and faithfulness to be motivated by duty. Instead, He wants to begin changing us on the inside through the love of Jesus. When His love is pouring into us, we cannot help but pour His love out to others, and that is the most important part of the calling we have been given.

"A new commandment I give to you, that you love one another, even as I have loved you, that you also love one another."

John 13:34

Allow the love of Jesus to really sink in—believe that He loves you as much as He says He does. Then, allow the Holy Spirit to lead you as He gives you the ability to love others the way He has loved you.

The servants at the wedding are willing to fill waterpots with water for a while, and because they do this, they witness a miraculous event. You may not understand God's work. It may seem like you are simply filling pots with water, but the work of the Lord is to seek and save the lost. God desires to fill those who are empty with living water so that they will never thirst again. When your belief begins to align with God's love, and you allow Him to work in and through you, you will see a miraculous transformation in the lives of those around you. You will see miracles.

- APPLICATION -

1. Is there any work or responsibility you believe God has given or asked you to do? How faithful have you been in that area? If you have a hard time being faithful, you may need to ask God to reset your motivation in that area. He asks us to love because He has loved us.

2. What strengths do you feel like God gave you? What are you most passionate about? Do you know that God made you unique for a reason?

3. Do you have a large ambition that you dream of completing in your lifetime? If you do, I encourage you to make sure that dream is not based in selfishness. Building our own kingdoms is meaningless in the end, but if we surrender our dreams to God, He can use them to change people's lives forever.

– FINAL THOUGHTS –

God does not want you to be miserable in your work for Him. I am not saying His work will never be hard to do, or that you will never experience failure, but you should not have to dread what God has called you to do. If you are experiencing dread or burnout in God's work, please do not just bear it. Take the time to hear God's voice and gain guidance for what you are doing. He can give you strength or insight to work with joy.

If you are working faithfully and yet feeling unloved, it may be time to rest and seek Him so that the Holy Spirit can remind you of how much God really does love you. This is how much He loves you: when you deserved punishment, Jesus took your punishment and gave you His righteousness. The only requirement He set for you to receive it is to believe in Jesus (see John 6:29). Remember, true belief in Christ does require a repentant attitude.

– DAY EIGHTEEN –
Come Home, Child

> "But the father said to his slaves, 'Quickly bring out the best robe and put it on him, and put a ring on his hand and sandals on his feet; and bring the fattened calf, kill it, and let us eat and celebrate; for this son of mine was dead and has come to life again; he was lost and has been found.'"
>
> Luke 15:22-24a

The story of Naaman in 2 Kings is a powerful testament of God's healing, but it can be easy to overlook a segment of the story that seems trivial. The sad truth was that Naaman was a leper, and nothing could cure him of his leprosy. It must have been a hopeful day when a servant girl from Israel told Naaman about a prophet in Israel that could heal him. Because of his need, Naaman left home and traveled to Israel. After meeting Elisha's messenger and being instructed to bathe seven times in the Jordan River, Naaman (with some persuasion) hesitantly decided to give it a try. Immediately after bathing, the leprosy was gone. He was finally clean.

It is no surprise that Naaman went straight to Elisha to thank him for his healing, and we get to read a snippet of their conversation in 2 Kings 5.

In verses 17 through 18, Naaman says,

"...If not, please let your servant at least be given two mules' load of earth; for your servant will no longer offer burnt offering nor will he sacrifice to other gods, but to the Lord. In this matter may the Lord pardon your servant: when my master goes into the house of Rimmon to worship there, and he leans on my hand and I bow myself in the house of Rimmon, when I bow myself in the house of Rimmon, the Lord pardon your servant in this matter."

Because Naaman experienced the power of God in his life, he turned to the Lord and declared that he was going to sacrifice only to the Lord God and to no other god. Naaman's life had been drastically changed. He saw the work of the Creator of the universe and he consequently made a pledge that he would only serve Him. However, after giving his speech about serving no other god except *the* God, Naaman makes a seemingly trivial concession. He says that even though God was Lord, he needed to be pardoned because he was still going to bow in the house of another god when his master went in to worship. Naaman basically said, "I'm giving my life completely to God, but there's just a little part of it that I'm too afraid to give up."

Sadly, Naaman reserved a small part of God's Lordship for himself, and I think we can often be tempted to do the same thing. When we are saved, God does a miracle in our lives. He takes all of our sin and shame away and washes us white as snow by the blood of Jesus Christ. When we first accept such a gift of grace, we are able to say, "Lord, take everything and make me a new creation."

Even though we are cleansed because of grace, that does not mean we are perfect in conduct. Thank God for His continued grace in our lives. When we mess up, it is important that we are able to receive conviction from the Holy Spirit and recognize our need for repentance. God knows that we are not perfect, and He knows that we are going to make mistakes. When we do, He gently wants to lead us to repentance and show us His grace. The Naaman-like temptation comes when we feel it would be okay to reserve a part of our sin from God. When we do this, we attempt to keep a part of His Lordship for our own.

In Jeremiah 3:6-10, God is talking through the prophet about the sins of Judah and Israel.

In verse 10, God says,

"Yet in spite of all this her treacherous sister Judah did not return to Me with all her heart, but rather in deception..."

It is easy to feel repentant in church, but we may leave that spirit of repentance and brokenness behind as soon as we walk out of those doors. It may be natural to have a humble attitude regarding sin when we are reading the Bible or talking about God's Word in a study group, but to allow God access to the deepest places of our hearts when we are in the *middle* of temptation can be difficult.

No matter what we think we are hiding from God, He knows everything about us, yet He loves us still. The key to having a humble, repentant attitude about our sin is to continuously rely on the love of Jesus that was shown to us on the cross. When you first came and kneeled at the cross, Jesus accepted you fully, giving you His own righteousness. No matter what mistakes you have made since then, His love for you has not changed. When you lay your sins at the foot of the cross and believe that He paid the price, His love fills your heart and gives you complete freedom from sin and shame *every* time.

It is the fear of God's possible response that causes some of us to shy away from honesty with Him about sin in our lives. Listen to this:

"There is no fear in love; but perfect love casts out fear, because fear involves punishment, and the one who fears is not perfected in love."

1 John 4:18

God's love casts out fear. We do not have to be afraid of punishment when we come to the cross and accept His grace, because Jesus took the punishment for all of our sin (past, present, and future) when He suffered and died on the cross. If the enemy ever tries to make you afraid of bringing your sin before the Lord, point the enemy to the blood of Jesus. Remind him that everything you owed has been paid in full.

If the prodigal son had only known what the Father's response would be, he would have returned home much sooner. I believe that God is saying to those who have been running, *it's time to come home again, child. It's time to come home, daughter. It's time to come home, son.* If you feel like you are hiding something from God, let me remind you that He already knows about it. God loves you, and He is the Father standing at the end of the road waiting for His child to run back into His open arms.

- APPLICATION -

1. When was the last time you asked God to search your heart? Is there a sin, even in your thoughts, that you have a hard time giving up? The answer is not to just try harder to stay pure. You may have already tried that! The answer is to come to God in repentance and surrender to the love and grace of Jesus Christ. His presence and power are what bring the change.

2. Do you have any recurring issues in your behavior, such as actions motivated by anger, fear, or hurt? Have you asked God to help you deal with it? Please do not be afraid to be honest with yourself and God.

– FINAL THOUGHTS –

One main reason we hold onto sin is because it is temporarily fun and comforting. Because of this, we may think God wants to keep us from having any fun. You may think, "It's just this one harmless sin. Everyone else has something that they do, why can't I?" This idea follows a false assumption that sin is more fun and comforting than anything God could give us in exchange. The truth is that God designed you, which means He knows exactly how to satisfy your desires. Comfort sins attempt to satisfy a deep desire that only God can completely satisfy. God wants you to be whole on the inside. Ask Him to fill that space with Himself and His good plan for you.

- DAY NINETEEN -
God's Wisdom and the Wisdom of Man

"Because the foolishness of God is wiser than men, and the weakness of God is stronger than men."

1 Corinthians 1:25

One time I had a critical decision to make that I kept running through in my mind. I would weigh the pros and cons, and talk it over with others, but I still felt stuck. Every time I attempted to reach a conclusion, I became highly agitated at my verdict. Finally, I sat down and prayed about it. I was convinced that the answer was either one way or the other. I was waiting for a definite *yes* or *no*, but when I took the issue before God, I discovered that His answers often involve more wisdom than mine. The answer I received was to simply wait.

Even as believers, we sometimes live in a continual state of unrest. What is so terrible about this fact is that some of us have reached the point where we consider it normal. When I had that important decision to make, I could not find peace in either direction. What I failed to realize was that I felt like I had to turn left or right, and God simply wanted me to come before Him. When I did that, I received a supernatural peace from Him that overpowered and overcame my distress. As I began trusting in His wisdom above my own, I found peace in the middle of the unresolved situation. I knew that, since He was present, everything would turn out for the best. Letting go of my own understanding in this certain situation was not easy, but it was certainly worth it.

Proverbs 3:13 says,

"How blessed is the man who finds wisdom and the man who gains understanding."

One time, a child wanted to buy a new bicycle that he had seen in a shop downtown. He had saved his money for months and was now able to purchase his new bike. He took his mother to the shop and pointed out the item, but to his surprise she said that he should wait and purchase it at a later date. He could not believe it! He had practiced extreme frugality, and now he expected a reward for his patience. No matter how he pleaded, his mother still advised him not to buy it just yet. Eventually, they left and he agreed to drop the subject. However, he later returned to the shop on his own, carrying his wallet full of the money he had saved. He walked up to the counter, slapped the money down, and announced that he wished to purchase the bike. He was so proud of himself, riding home on his new bicycle. When he arrived, he realized he would have to hide it or else his mother would know what he had done. In the garage, he found an old tarp draped over some boxes in the corner. He pulled back the tarp, and to his surprise he found an identical bike, wrapped with ribbon and a bow. Written on an attached card were the words, "Happy Birthday, son. Enjoy your new bike!"

The boy in the story thought that his mother's advice sounded rather foolish. He had determinedly saved and waited. He could not understand why his mother would tell him to wait when *he* had already decided that it was time. Often, God's wisdom is not going to make a lot of sense to us. The reason is because He knows everything, and we know only what we can see in front of us. Though our wisdom sounds good in the moment, it can never outmatch the wisdom of an all-knowing, loving Creator.

The question we sometimes have when we are waiting for something is, "Does God really know the best timing for this?" The truth is that God knows everything. The question we should really be asking ourselves is, "Do I really believe God loves me as much as He says He does?" A perfectly loving God is going to provide for His children at the best time, and in the best way.

In Job 38, God speaks of His wisdom and might in creating the earth and all that is in it.

He says in verse 4,

"Where were you when I laid the foundation of the earth? Tell Me, if you have understanding."

God is making a clear distinction between His wisdom and the wisdom of man. It is very difficult to read the later chapters of Job and still think man has any wisdom when it comes to understanding God's ways. Our wisdom is nothing compared to His, but the wonderful thing about this is His plans are for our good. That means that we do not have to have everything figured out! We simply need to trust in Him.

God showed us the ultimate example of His wisdom and love working hand-in-hand when He sent Jesus to die for us. In fact, He even tells us in His Word that His salvation plan will not make complete sense to our natural minds. Paul writes about the spiritual wisdom behind God's plan for salvation, and how the power of God that makes a change in our lives is wrapped up in believing the simple gospel message.

Paul says it like this:

"...so that your faith would not rest on the wisdom of men, but on the power of God."

1 Corinthians 2:5

The gift of salvation and freedom in Christ may seem foolish when we examine it with our own wisdom, but this is God's plan. His desire is not for us to presently understand everything; His desire is that we will believe what He has said to us. Thankfully, when we act in faith, we get to see His hand at work.

How does this truth apply to your current situation? God desires to take care of us and make us fruitful. He promised to provide all that we need in His Word. The mother in the story told her son to wait because she had good plans in store for him. Similarly, God wants us to trust Him as we wait for His good plans.

Proverbs 3:5-6 says,

"Trust in the Lord with all your heart and do not lean on your own understanding. In all your ways acknowledge Him, and He will make your paths straight."

You can trust in the Lord because His character is one of faithfulness. The same loving Father who provided salvation for us while we were still sinners will provide for our needs at the perfect time as we fully place our trust in Him.

- APPLICATION -

1. When you are faced with difficult decisions, do you wait in prayer for the Lord to give direction?

2. Do you find it easier to ask God for wisdom with everyday scenarios or with big decisions? Why?

3. Why do you think it is so important to trust that the descriptions of God's character in the Bible are true?

- FINAL THOUGHTS -

If we are not careful, prayer time can become a chance to deliver our "to-do" list to God. God does care about our needs, and the Bible tells us to let our requests be known to God. However, if we only ever tell God what to do, then we will never hear what He wants us to do. We need to trust Him that He has a good plan in mind.

Take the time to be quiet before God, and learn to hear His still, quiet voice. If you do, you will find He has more to say than just telling you which direction to take.

- DAY TWENTY -
Cleaning House

"Search me, O God, and know my heart; Try me and know my anxious thoughts; And see if there be any hurtful way in me, And lead me in the everlasting way."

Psalms 139:23-24

Have you ever invited a friend over only to realize that your house needed some major help in the cleaning department? When this happens, I find myself deciding which rooms need cleaning and which rooms can stay messy because most of the time I do not invite people into every room of my house. The living room and common areas end up clean while the other rooms sometimes still look like wrecks. In the worst cases, clothes and items are lying out, the floors are not swept, and the mirrors are unwashed. When time is limited, I only clean the rooms that I know visitors will see.

This makes me think about the fact that without Jesus, each of our lives is like a messy house. The dust that comes with time is everywhere. Dirty mistakes clutter the floor, stains of sinful living are highly evident, and as far as we know, there is no hope of restoring things back to the way they were meant to be. What is our natural reaction? It can be embarrassing for people to see us in such a state, so we clean house the best that we know how. We shuffle items out of the living area and into the rest of the house. We go to church, putting our best face on so people will think everything is in order, but the truth is the rest of the house is in a state of pure chaos. We can hang out with our Christian friends and talk about Christian things while the other rooms in our life are filled with a different subject matter altogether. What we may overlook is that God does not need our permission to look into the other rooms. No matter what you or I have tried to sweep under the rug, God knows it is there. Fortunately for us, He has a cleaning solution that is unmatched by any product the world will try to sell you off the shelves.

You see, God knew our lives would be messy. After looking through time and seeing the state of things, He knew there was no way we would ever be able to clean house by ourselves. Have you ever watched the show *Dirty Jobs*? It is all about certain types of jobs that are so dirty, most people would not be able to handle them. Well, God sent the Master Cleaner to do the dirty job that no one else had the ability to do. That job was cleaning us up. If you are a believer, that means Jesus came knocking on your door with His cleaning supplies in hand. When Jesus cleans house, He does a perfect job. Yes, it takes time, but He finishes what He starts. We leave a few rooms undone, or we sweep the dirt under the rug. In contrast, Jesus makes everything spotless. He vacuums, shampoos and steams the carpet, waxes the floor, and removes any collecting garbage. However, there is a catch that I need to mention:

"In this is love, not that we loved God, but that He loved us and sent His Son to be the propitiation for our sins."

1 John 4:10

Jesus knew that we would not be able to afford the price of the cleaning solution He had to offer, and so He paid the price Himself. Now He says, *This is a gift. It's free of charge, but in order for Me to make you spotless, you've got to do something. You've got to let me in. You've got to let me see the whole house.* Jesus does not just barge in; He enters only by invitation. If you have believed in Him, then you have at one point allowed Jesus to enter into your heart and become the Lord of your life. When you let Him in, you were made spotless—white like snow. Like many of us, maybe over the years you have started to collect dust. There may be some rooms that are not in order anymore—some areas of life that you have allowed sin to rule. When this happens, it can be tempting to close the door of your heart to Jesus. Let me remind you that God already knows the state of things. He is simply waiting for you to open every door, confess, and show Him your deepest and darkest basement. When you do this, He then reminds you, *I already consider you clean, because your cleanliness is based on the righteousness of Jesus. The price is still paid in full. My love for you has not changed, and the reason I want to continue to work on you is because I want the very best for you.*

- APPLICATION -

1. Read 2 Corinthians 5:17. Have you ever asked Jesus to make you a new person on the inside?

2. Is there any area of your life you are afraid to let Jesus see? Remember that love covers a multitude of sins.

- FINAL THOUGHTS -

God is not a mean, cosmic police officer, waiting to punish us for our mistakes. He is the Great Physician, working to heal us completely. He also wants to make us like Christ through the Holy Spirit working in our hearts. There is no reason to try to hide the junk in our lives from Him. It is actually what is really hurting us, and His desire is for us to be healed and whole people.

– DAY TWENTY-ONE –
A Treasure of Great Worth

"For the kingdom of God is not eating and drinking, but righteousness and peace and joy in the Holy Spirit."

Romans 14:17

There are times in my Christian walk when I truly desire to be doing what God wants, but for some reason, I have temporarily lost my passion for His kingdom. I still long to please Him, but at the same time, I find it difficult to feel the same excitement that I once felt about furthering the kingdom. It is easy to believe that when we feel this way, we have somehow failed God. This thought can even begin to further hinder our relationship with Him. If what I am talking about sounds familiar to you, I have some good news: God's Word gives us the answer, and it is better than you might think.

Jesus says in Matthew 13:44,

"The kingdom of heaven is like a treasure hidden in the field, which a man found and hid again; and from joy over it he goes and sells all that he has and buys that field."

Jesus tells a parable about a man who is full of passion over what he discovers, and we see his excitement and joy displayed in his actions. Why does he sell everything that he owns to get the field? When he looks at the field, he does not see the sacrifice it takes to sell everything he has. He does not see the work it takes to bury the treasure and dig it back up again. Instead, he sees the *worth* of the treasure that is buried there.

In the following verses, Matthew 13:45-46, Jesus segues into another short parable:

"Again, the kingdom of heaven is like a merchant seeking fine pearls, and upon finding one pearl of great value, he went and sold all that he had and bought it."

In both parables, the treasure is equated with the kingdom. Do you know why we lose our passion for the kingdom? I believe it is often because we start focusing on the work involved, and we take our eyes off of the worth of the treasure we have been given. The worth of the kingdom is this: Jesus, the Son of God, lived a perfect life and then allowed Himself to be crucified for our sins. We are able now and for eternity to come confidently into God's presence, knowing we are righteous in His eyes because of the blood of Jesus. If we could see the kingdom for what it really is, we would be willing to go and sell everything in order to get it.

I have a coin collection, and the joy of coin collecting comes in knowing the worth of each piece. If you collect coins, you know what it is like to find a coin of great value. When you get it, you treat it differently than the other coins in the collection. Out of excitement, you place it in the most expensive case, and you display it in the most visited part of the house. When we do not value the treasure of the kingdom at its worth, we let our calling as believers fall into place alongside all the other priorities in our lives. If someone asked you where in your life the kingdom could be found, would you have to shuffle through a box of old coins to find it? Would it be on display like the treasure it is?

Some of us have made the kingdom of heaven about marriage or dating. Some of us have made it about attending church. Some of us have made the kingdom about Christian music or events. We may have even made it about acts of kindness or trying our hardest to love people. When we begin to think that our value in God's eyes is based on our performance, we miss the gift of God. Because of His love, He determined your value once and for all by giving His Son in exchange for you.

1 Corinthians 1:18 says,

"For the word of the cross is foolishness to those who are perishing, but to us who are being saved it is the power of God."

The worth of the kingdom is in the power of the gospel. When you first enter the kingdom, the power of God begins to completely transform your life, making you a new creation. You begin to grow into an image of Christ, something that would have been impossible to do alone. The great worth is in the power, and the power of God is *not* found in going to church. It is not found in doing "spiritually mature" things. The power of God is found only in the cross. It is found in continuously believing that His grace is sufficient. As we abide in the love of Jesus, and allow the Holy Spirit to mold us, those other things come automatically because He is doing the work in us.

When you live in light of the belief that a perfect God loved sinners so much that He purposefully sent His only begotten Son to die in our stead, you experience the transforming power of God in your life. Then the kingdom suddenly becomes something worth being passionate about because its eternal value outweighs everything else that we own.

- APPLICATION -

1. How much of a priority is the kingdom of God in your life? Is your kingdom motivation rising from a desire to perform, or are you daily trusting in the work Jesus?

2. Are you experiencing Jesus' transforming power in your life? Have you witnessed the results of abiding in Christ on a daily basis?

- FINAL THOUGHTS -

If you are a believer, God's kingdom is where you will ultimately live for all eternity. As believers, we are supposed to experience what it is like to be operating in that kingdom here on earth. You can spend your whole life becoming an expert on the things of the world, but when your life is over, you may find that it was a waste of time. I am not saying that everything in life should be shunned, but I am saying that your priorities matter when it comes to receiving the Christ-like character God desires to create in you. I encourage you to become an expert in the ways of the kingdom of God. Only in His kingdom is there the power to positively impact lives for eternity.

– DAY TWENTY-TWO –
A Key to Every Door

"Be anxious for nothing, but in everything by prayer and supplication with thanksgiving let your requests be made known to God."

Philippians 4:6

You have probably heard honeymoon disaster stories involving traveling mishaps. When my wife and I took our honeymoon, the idea that our week long vacation together could turn into one of those stories never entered my mind. As far as the trip arrangements were concerned, everything seemed to be going as planned right up to the last day. We stayed in a beautiful cabin in the hills of Tennessee, and we went hiking up mountains almost every day. The night before our departure, we swept up, packed, and got everything ready for leaving. Waking up early in the AM, we made sure to lock the key inside the cabin as instructed. Then we drove an hour to the airport in our rental car, tired after our adventure.

The airport was nearly empty that early in the morning, so we deposited the rental car key and papers in an unmanned drop-off bin. Besides being sleepy, everything seemed to be normal until we reached the ticket desk. It was the only time I have ever heard a check-in assistant say, "I'm sorry. That flight does not exist." My wife and I both stood there, wondering what the lady could possibly mean. She quickly found the flight we were scheduled to take and informed us that it was scheduled for the same time the next day. As I pondered what the ramifications of arriving a day early to the airport would be, I suddenly felt locked out.

What do I mean by that? We had one more day left on our car rental schedule, and we had one more day left to enjoy our cabin, but now we had no way of getting into either of them. We had mistakenly showed up to the airport a day early, and now we were stuck at the airport with no car, no cabin, and our traveling money had mostly been spent. I am sure as I sat there, feeling rather silly and upset at myself, that I mumbled a half-hearted prayer that sounded something like this: "How do you plan on getting us out of this one, God?"

Is that not how we pray sometimes? When life locks us out, and there is no solution that can solve our problem, we often mumble insincere prayers that really sound more like complaints about how God has failed to come through. The reason these kinds of prayers are weak prayers is because they are not prayers spoken in faith.

I am not saying that being tired and stuck in an airport is the worst thing that can happen. However, we can use this scenario as a picture of where a lot of us find ourselves in life—tired and stuck. Maybe you are going through an emotional hardship, or maybe you are trapped in a financial bind, or perhaps there is a health crisis to which you have no solution. Whatever the problem may be, all of us sometimes find ourselves locked out by life.

Despite my attitude, God lovingly heard my prayer. After a while of just sitting and waiting, I suddenly reached down and felt something in my pocket. I pulled it out to find that I still had the rental car key. In my tired state, I had forgotten to place it in the envelope with the rental papers when I slipped it in the bin. We had one key out of two, and so we decided that we would drive back to the cabin and try to find a way in. It was an hour drive, and we were not sure if we would be able to get back in, but at least we were taking a small step in faith. When you are stepping out in faith, that is when the serious praying starts. It could have been a bust, and we could have been stuck napping in the car out in the freezing weather. But as we drove, I prayed, this time believing that God would give us a way in.

When you pray with authority, your prayers begin to sound more like declarations than complaints. Praying in faith does not mean that you always see immediate results. It means that you pray in connection to God's Word and His Spirit. If you are tired of prayers that lack faith, the solution is a renewed authority through Christ. We receive authority by abiding in Jesus. As we seek Him, He fills us with the Holy Spirit and with power.

In Luke 10:19, Jesus makes His followers aware of their influential position. He says,

"Behold, I have given you authority to tread on serpents and scorpions, and over all the power of the enemy, and nothing will injure you."

When my wife and I arrived at our cabin, I climbed the icy balcony and found that the second story door we had trouble closing properly all week could be opened from the outside. We showed up, and God made a way in. We quickly went from having no keys and no way in to having both a rental car and a cabin for what we considered an extra day.

As I said, I am using this story as a picture. There is a reason God allows us to get stuck in life: so we will begin to seek Him in faith. God knows we are better off seeking Him in a trial than being anywhere else or seeking anything else. I encourage you to seek Jesus with your whole heart today. It takes a step of faith, but you can do it with His help.

Jesus says in Matthew 11:28,

"Come to Me, all who are weary and heavy-laden, and I will give you rest."

Oftentimes, we grow weary and then forget to come to Jesus for rest. Sometimes, we are even running away from God because we feel like we have failed Him. Feeling like a failure may cause us to wait until the last minute to bring our issues to God. Remember, God did not wait for us to change before He sent His Son as a sacrifice for our sins. He loved us so much that He decided to be proactive about saving us. He had already paid the price for you and me before we were even born. When we choose to walk in belief, we can bring our struggles, hardships, and even mistakes before our loving Father in faith, knowing that He hears us and His love will cover us. He will be there to lift us up during the hardships and to restore us when we make mistakes. When we abide in Jesus, we discover that God holds the keys to every door we need to open.

Isaiah 55:6-7 beautifully describes God's response to us, so I want to leave you with these words:

"Seek the Lord while He may be found; Call upon Him while He is near. Let the wicked forsake his way And the unrighteous man his thoughts; And let him return to the Lord, And He will have compassion on him, And to our God, For He will abundantly pardon."

- APPLICATION -

1. Do you feel tired or stuck in any situation right now? Remember, God is faithful. He has not forgotten about you. If you ever feel like He has, read Isaiah 49:15.

2. Do you take hardships to God as they come, or do you wait till the problems get bigger to ask Him for help? God cares about even the little things in your life. You can trust Him to help you.

3. Are your prayer requests full of faith, or do they resemble complaints full of doubt? Because of the blood of Jesus, you can come confidently before Him in prayer.

- FINAL THOUGHTS -

Faith can be built as you continue to walk with God. If you can think back and remember the great things God has done in your life, you will be more likely to trust Him in the future rather than doubt. The next time you find yourself in a sticky situation, it might be worth writing down everything God has delivered you from in the past. If you do not feel like you have a strong history with God, you can "borrow" someone else's. In other words, I encourage you to allow the testimonies of how God has moved in other people's lives to strengthen your faith. You can pray and trust God to move similarly in your own life.

– DAY TWENTY-THREE –
A Friend for the Road

"You have taken account of my wanderings; Put my tears in Your bottle. Are they not in Your book?"

Psalm 56:8

I often watched *Winnie the Pooh* cartoons as a young child, and my favorite film staring that gang of lovable, stuffed characters was *Pooh's Grand Adventure: The Search for Christopher Robin*. I loved this film more than the others because of the adventure, excitement, and danger that the stuffed animal friends faced. If you have ever seen *Winnie the Pooh*, then you know that Pooh is not the brightest of bears. Whenever he finds himself in a pickle, he relies on the wisdom of his owner and friend, a young boy named Christopher Robin. In this particular favorite of mine, Pooh and his friends discover a letter from Christopher Robin that informs them where he has gone and that he will return. Because the animals do not take very good care of the letter, they end up misreading it and eventually embark on an unnecessary grand adventure to find their friend.

During their journey, they face fearful obstacles and perils that keep them from reaching their destination, and they often feel like giving up. When I think about this childhood favorite that I used to watch, it reminds me of my life. God gave us the amazing gift of wisdom through His Word, but while we may have many translations, it can be easy to misread the message. In the movie, Pooh and his friends even go so far as to, figuratively, read between the lines. When I open up God's Word, only looking to hear what I want to hear, I can do the same thing. It is not until we open our hearts to hear what God is truly saying that we can be shaped into the vessels He desires to create.

Along their way, Pooh and his friends come up against a massive gorge, a forest of thorns, dark caves, and other dangers. When I think about this journey, I think about my life, and I remember the forests and caves that I have already gone through. An interesting thing happens in the film. Once Pooh and his friends finally reach their destination, they are reunited with Christopher Robin, and they all begin to make the return journey. On the way home, everything that had at first appeared impossible to overcome now seems small and even trivial. Why?

The first time they passed through the dangers, they walked alone. The second time, their owner walked with them. Life has a way of attempting to overwhelm us with one obstacle or impossibility after the next. When we are walking alone, it can be natural to give fear and discouragement a place in our hearts. However, when God walks with us, we see the obstacles not as they appear to us, but rather as they appear to Him.

God has set us on a grand adventure, and He has given us a map, or letter, to help us along the way. When we read between the lines, or imagine we can keep ourselves on track better than He can, we quickly find ourselves overwhelmed, wondering why God is not there. At the beginning of the film, Christopher Robin encourages Pooh with the line, "Even if we're apart, I'll always be with you." God has said something very similar in His Word.

Hebrews 13:5b says,

"For He Himself has said, 'I will never desert you, nor will I ever forsake you.'"

Even when we feel the most alone, God has never truly deserted us. The reason we know that God will not forsake us is because He paid a heavy price to ransom us from the clutches of death. Because of sin, we were all on a path that led straight to eternal separation from God. Loving us perfectly, God sent Jesus to bear the punishment for our sins.

That is how much God desires to be with us. He also desires an intimate relationship with us as we journey through this life, and we engage in this relationship by abiding in His love. It is His love that encourages us to be led by the Holy Spirit, to hide His Word in our hearts, and to keep seeking Him first. As His love becomes our motivation, we start to see Him in our circumstances and we begin to see the path ahead through His eyes.

- APPLICATION -

1. When you read God's Word, do you ask God to speak to you through it? Remember, His voice is still and small.

2. Do you ever feel alone? Remember, God has not simply left you here with a list of instructions. He did not send you on a solo mission to see if you will succeed. The Holy Spirit wants to walk with you every day.

- FINAL THOUGHTS -

There is a grand adventure that God wants to take you on. Because He is a good Father, He wants to walk beside you. He desires to be close and spend time with you. He is not so interested in how much you can accomplish on your own. He is more interested in you and Him being together for the journey.

- DAY TWENTY-FOUR -
Solving Finances God's Way

"For where your treasure is, there your heart will be also."

Matthew 6:21

One day, I was attempting to make some progress on a jigsaw puzzle that my wife and I had been working on for several weeks. I gathered all the pieces I could find of a certain color and pattern, hoping to complete that section of the puzzle. As I struggled to fit the pieces together, I began to grow irritated. I had found all of the pieces that looked alike, and I had tried for several minutes to combine them in different ways. None of the pieces seemed to go together. So, out of frustration, I pulled the box full of puzzle pieces out and began to look for more pieces. I figured if the ones I had did not fit together, then I must not have enough pieces. And as I began to add more and more pieces to the lot, I became even more upset. It seems that adding more is not always the solution.

Though money is a necessity, I do not think it is always the solution we need. I believe that our finances are in many ways like a puzzle. When the issues begin to grow and we feel more and more irritated by what life is handing us, we can think that the answer is simply to gather more money. It is frustrating to feel like nothing you are doing is working. What we have tried so far is not fitting together, and so we may assume that the answer is to get more. When that does not work, we go back to the box of life, searching yet again for even more.

The more puzzle pieces that I pulled out of the box, the more confused I was. I did not grow less irritated; I grew more irritated. How often do we read about wealthy people whose lives have been destroyed even though they had plenty of money? Those stories still fail to persuade us against putting our hope in wealth. I am not saying money is intrinsically bad. However, how we view and use our money can have a weighty effect on our lives.

While I was attempting to put together the puzzle, the answer was not to go searching for more pieces. The answer was to first figure out how to fit together the pieces I already had. God has a whole box of puzzle pieces. He has a treasury so full that we could never even begin to imagine it. Before He is going to bring us an increase out of His box, He wants to see what we are going to do with what He has already placed in our hands.

Jesus says in Luke 6:38:

"Give, and it will be given to you. They will pour into your lap a good measure—pressed down, shaken together, and running over. For by your standard of measure it will be measured to you in return."

God desires us, as His adored children, to be givers. He wants us to ultimately create a picture—to be image bearers of God. When we allow His love to motivate our financial choices, we put our pieces together to form a picture of His Son. The world does not need to see another financial success. The world needs to see the love, generosity, and kindheartedness of Jesus. God's desire is that we will live every day using the resources He has given us to become reflections of Him.

I know money can be a touchy subject. I have been in situations where I had no idea how my wife and I were going to make payments. However, I also know that I have been changed by the love of God. God does not want you to buck up and give out of a sense of duty—His goal is to give you a cheerful heart. God's desire is that the love of Jesus will fill your heart through the work of the Holy Spirit so much that your heart will spout generosity. God reveals His plan to shape our motivation in this verse:

"We love, because He first loved us."

1 John 4:19

God wants us to be generous, not to earn blessings, but out of response to His giving. When we were sinful people, God generously sent His Son to die in our place. He did this because of His great love for us. The God who loved us that much also wants to provide for our every need. Jesus makes a good promise in Matthew 6:33:

"But seek first His kingdom and His righteousness, and all these things will be added to you."

- APPLICATION -

1. How does the way you use your money portray God to others? Have you allowed His love to motivate you?

2. In what ways could you be more faithful in the little things when it comes to your finances?

- FINAL THOUGHTS -

Jesus talked about money more than anything else during His ministry. This may be because having money is essential to life. It takes time and effort to earn money. We literally trade days of our lives for money. It is amazing that Jesus traded His life completely for ours. Through giving, we get to paint a picture of His love.

- DAY TWENTY-FIVE -
What's in a Name?

> "So this I say, and affirm together with the Lord, that you walk no longer just as the Gentiles also walk, in the futility of their mind, being darkened in their understanding, excluded from the life of God because of the ignorance that is in them, because of the hardness of their heart."
>
> Ephesians 4:17-18

One morning, I prepared to go on a walk before work. As I sat on my front porch tying my shoes, I noticed a gray woodpecker swoop down over the yard and land atop a metal electricity pole. He sat on a plastic cover at the apex of the metal pole, staring intently at the object on which he perched. I began to think out loud, saying, "There's no way he's going to try to peck that." Just as I finished saying it, the woodpecker began to hammer forcefully at the plastic. You can guess that his attempt to peck the plastic failed because of the metal underneath.

Picking his head up and shaking off, he tried once more, but again with no luck. As I watched him hurt himself by attempting to peck something that was not meant to be pecked, I realized that we probably all have done something similar. You see, a woodpecker is made with a purpose—to peck wood. He was given a unique beak and bone structure so that he can peck holes into wood and eat the bugs inside. Every one of us is designed with a purpose. God has given us specific gifts, talents, and abilities to be used for furthering His kingdom in specific ways. When we get too caught up in the gifts or tools that we have, we miss out on the reason behind the design—we miss the purposes for which we were made.

Ephesians 2:10 says,

"For we are His workmanship, created in Christ Jesus for good works, which God prepared beforehand so that we would walk in them."

No matter how much he tries to peck at strange materials, that woodpecker is still a woodpecker. He is not a plastic pecker or a metal pecker. He is a woodpecker. It is amazing how he is named appropriately for his purpose. We who are in Christ have also been given a name appropriate for our purpose. We carry the name of Christ around in the title "Christian." Because He is the One who is living in us, we should continuously be becoming more Christ-like. Our identity is tied to our purpose.

Do you ever align your identity with other things? It is natural to try to copy the look of a celebrity, act like a favorite athlete, or sound like a notable band. Some of us attempt to be as successful as an influential business leader we look up to. Respecting someone is not bad, but centering your identity anywhere other than Christ can cause you to miss your purpose.

2 Timothy 1:9 says that God

"...has saved us and called us with a holy calling, not according to our works, but according to His own purpose and grace which was granted us in Christ Jesus from all eternity."

God's purpose for us looks different than the purpose we naturally choose for ourselves. He has a higher calling and identity in mind for us. Through Jesus Christ's work on the cross, God purchased our righteousness, giving us new identities in Christ. We receive that gift through faith. God did this because He loves us, but God does not just love believers. Jesus died for everyone because God loves all people with a perfect love. This is why His purpose for us involves sharing the good news with others. That is the *good work* (Ephesians 2:10) that Jesus has given us, and our motivation should not be to impress people or to earn points with God. Our motivation for sharing the gospel should be the belief that Jesus did the finished work for us on the cross.

If that woodpecker always pecks at the wrong materials, he will eventually starve to death because he will not be getting the sustenance he needs. If we only use our gifts to reach our dreams, at the end of the day we will still be spiritually empty. Paul lets us know in Ephesians 2:7 why God changes our identities, and it is because God desires us to find everything we need in Him.

"so that in the ages to come He might show the surpassing riches of His grace in kindness toward us in Christ Jesus."

- APPLICATION -

1. What is the source of your identity?

2. Have you asked God to show you your spiritual gifts?

- FINAL THOUGHTS -

You are a spiritual being, so your purpose is also spiritual. The more you allow God (by grace) to establish you as His loved child, the more His love will flow out of you to work His purposes.

- DAY TWENTY-SIX -
Why is Being a Christian so Hard?

"He gives strength to the weary, And to him who lacks might He increases power. Though youths grow weary and tired, And vigorous young men stumble badly, Yet those who wait for the Lord Will gain new strength; They will mount up with wings like eagles, They will run and not get tired."

Isaiah 40:29-31a

When I was in college, two friends asked if I would be willing to compete alongside them in a team triathlon. One of my friends competed as the runner, the other took the role of swimmer, and I was left to do the biking. Being a natural athlete, I agreed without a second thought. Casual bicycling had always been a breeze for me, and the event only included a short, twelve-mile track. The day of the race came and I started off without much of a problem. I had borrowed a cheap bicycle from a friend, and it took me the first stretch to figure out how to shift gears. About a mile in, however, I began thinking about how long it had been since I had last taken a solid bike ride. It must have been a good six months or more. Pushing myself, I soon reached an energetic peak. I was actually beginning to feel like a pro until something suddenly whizzed past me at a rapid pace. It was moving so fast that I hardly had time to notice. It was another rider.

From then on, the race went downhill. About two miles in, the chilly gust began to freeze my legs. It felt like riding through a snowstorm, and the short exercise shorts and tank top did not help. Then the cramps came, and they came hard. I leapt off the bike and grasped my side. Finding a nearby picnic table, I rested on top of it and attempted to catch my breath. I must have laid there for several minutes, listening to the peaceful sounds of the other cyclists zooming past. I thought to myself, *If they can do it, so can I.* So I jumped up, more determined than ever to finish strong.

I biked harder and harder. About halfway through the race, my left calf decided to seize up in the most painful cramp I have ever felt. Ten minutes later, I was back at it again, this time only pushing as hard as I dared without risking another cramp. The rest of the race felt like hours. It may have been. Finally, I neared the last hill. Filling with hope, I pushed myself once more. Then, my right leg decided that it was its turn to cramp up. I cringed. With burning legs, a sore body, and a beaten will, I stepped off the bicycle. After facing so much agony, I ended the race at only a fraction of the pace at which I began. I walked my bike up the final hill.

Have you ever considered why it is sometimes so hard to be a Christian? It can be easy to start something new for the kingdom of God, only to feel like giving up soon afterwards. When I started that race, I never assumed it would be difficult. My problem did not have to do with my natural athletic ability, energy levels, or passion to finish. The problem I was facing was plain and simple: I was not a cyclist.

Some of us are trying our hardest to live for the Lord, but we are doing it in our own strength. God does not want us to drain ourselves for His kingdom. He wants to change who we are. Once our identities transform, the rest comes naturally. If I had been a cyclist, I would have easily conquered those twelve miles. When we *become* little Christs through faith, His life dwells in us. God wants to put Jesus inside of us, so that when times get hard, Jesus' strength carries us. Look at what Galatians 2:20 says:

"I have been crucified with Christ; and it is no longer I who live, but Christ lives in me; and the life which I now live in the flesh I live by faith in the Son of God, who loved me and gave Himself up for me."

We receive Christ as our new source of strength and identity in life by believing in His loving sacrifice on the cross. Through the work of the Holy Spirit in us, He is able to accomplish through us what we could not do on our own. It is nice to know that our spiritual progress does not rest on our own effort. In a sense, God has even given us a "spiritual trainer" to walk with us. We know the Holy Spirit is a good gift because of the words of Jesus in John 14:16-17:

"I will ask the Father, and He will give you another Helper, that He may be with you forever; that is the Spirit of truth, whom the world cannot receive, because it does not see Him or know Him, but you know Him because He abides with you and will be in you."

- APPLICATION -

1. Are you fueled by accomplishments or love? Why?

2. Read about the work of the Spirit in Romans 5:5. Have you asked Jesus to fill you with the Holy Spirit?

- FINAL THOUGHTS -

We can treat churches like spiritual gyms we attend once or twice a week. Just showing up to a gym is not going to get us into shape, but I believe we can think that showing up to church is going to get us spiritually fit. Church is a good thing, but the greatest motivator is the love of Jesus. It is His grace and love that change us.

– DAY TWENTY-SEVEN –
A Change of Clothes

"...[P]resent your bodies a living and holy sacrifice, acceptable to God, which is your spiritual service of worship. And do not be conformed to this world, but be transformed by the renewing of your mind, so that you may prove what the will of God is, that which is good and acceptable and perfect."

Romans 12:1b-2

I told you about the struggle we had reading bedtime stories to my daughter, Mirabelle, when she was a baby. We often faced a similar issue when it came to changing her clothes. Every morning when she woke up and every night before she went to bed, we would change her little outfit. A few more changes per day were sometimes necessary depending on how much of a mess she made. Though Mirabelle was normally blessed with a sweet spirit, she did not care much for getting her clothes changed. I once thought that she probably would not mind wearing the same onesie twenty-four seven. As she pushed, cried, and attempted to free herself from such a seemingly unnecessary situation, Mirabelle never understood what she was actually doing. You see, when she stopped to take a breath and ceased her revolt for a moment, her mother and I were actually able to finish the job. Little did she know, it was the fight she put up that made the change last so long.

God loves His children very much. When you enter into the family of God, an immediate change takes place. You are transformed into a new creation as you are brought from a place of darkness to one of light. Although this change takes place, you and I both know that salvation does not mean perfection in our performance. We entered the family *by* grace, and we get to continue *in* grace.

You can be saved, set free, and gifted in the righteousness of God through Christ Jesus, but God still desires to make you even more like Jesus. I thank God that *He* is the One working to make those changes inside of us. However, because of pride or fear, we sometimes reject the work of the Holy Spirit in our lives. When we choose to fight the renewal process God desires for us, we are acting just like baby Mirabelle. God knows all things. He loves us unconditionally, and He showed this love by sending His Son to die for us. He knows what is best, even when we do not. We need to see that the struggle we put up against God's work in our hearts can make the process longer than He desires.

Philippians 1:6 says,

"For I am confident of this very thing, that He who began a good work in you will perfect it until the day of Christ Jesus."

My wife and I love Mirabelle too much to let her sit around in a filthy outfit all day. Similarly, God loves you too much to give up on you, no matter how you struggle.

I believe one of the hardest things we face when God is working on us is hearing truth spoken in love by a friend. It is okay when a pastor gets up onstage and speaks the Word of God, but when someone we are close to confronts us in love, that can be another story. When God uses those around you to point you towards Him, I encourage you to bring their words before the Lord in prayer. You can confirm that God is speaking through another believer by reading the Word of God and listening to the voice of the Holy Spirit.

Proverbs 27:17 says,

"Iron sharpens iron, So one man sharpens another."

Though it may hurt, the people pointing you to Christ are present because God means for us to sharpen one another. They are not perfect, and it takes humility to listen. If you do not see it now, I pray that someday it will be plain that God was speaking into your life through others believers. Children grow to understand that the good things we do for them are out of love. So, if you are in a rough spot, and God is working on your heart, focus on the loving work Jesus did for you on the cross. When His love fills your heart, it is easy to let Him continue the work.

- APPLICATION -

1. Do you think the Holy Spirit has finished molding you to be like Jesus, or do you think He still has more work to do? What is God speaking to you right now?

2. Do you have people in your life you trust to challenge you spiritually? If not, consider finding a strong Christian friend who can pray with and encourage you. You may not feel like it, but you can encourage them too.

- FINAL THOUGHTS -

Feeling uncomfortable can be a sign of growth. As humans, it is natural for us to try placing ourselves in the most comfortable positions we can and avoid any kind of discomfort. The problem is, in a place of worldly comfort, we never grow. If God asks you to do something uncomfortable, remember that He desires to be your comfort. In John 14:16, Jesus even calls the Holy Spirit our Comforter (KJV). I encourage you to allow Him to help, comfort, and counsel you.

DAY TWENTY-EIGHT

The Desire to Be a Hero

> "More than that, I count all things to be loss in view of the surpassing value of knowing Christ Jesus my Lord, for whom I have suffered the loss of all things, and count them but rubbish so that I may gain Christ."
>
> Philippians 3:8

As a man, I have always had an insatiable desire to be a hero. Even from a young age, I dreamed of one day being recognized for a heroic deed or a feat of greatness. As I took on the role of an adult, instead of realizing this dream, I was met with disappointment. The older I became, the more I began believing that a hero was only someone from a story or legend. I am not saying that heroes do not exist. There are many people alive today that I would label as heroes. However, as I grew into adulthood, I assumed that I would never be one of them. For a while, I gave up on the idea of becoming a hero.

One of my favorite animated films is *The Iron Giant*. It is the story of a boy who discovers an enormous robot and begins teaching him what it is like to be human. As a child watching this film, I immediately related to the boy. What child would not love to find a robot that wants to be his friend? For a while, I thought the film was about the experience of becoming friends with a robot. It was not until I became a man that I saw the film differently.

I watched the film again as an adult. My association with the boy had changed so that I suddenly related more to the giant robot. The robot was faced with a choice that I believe every man and woman faces. Deep down, his programming told him that he was meant to destroy, but love told him something different. As humans, we were born with a sin nature that tries to rule and lead us down a path of destruction, but we received a new nature in Christ when we were born again. As I first transitioned into manhood, I found myself feeling like a confused giant compared to my childhood self. For a while, I allowed myself to be led by destructive programming that I thought I could not avoid. It was not until God introduced me to the love of Jesus that I was able to choose a better way.

The Iron Giant finds himself faced with a choice, and he eventually decides to lay aside his natural programming to save the ones he loves. I believe that to be heroes, we are not required to perform heroic acts for thousands of people. We do not have to be firefighters, soldiers, or surgeons to impact lives. Heroic acts are good, but being true heroes starts with being heroes to the people around us. God wants us to start there.

Paul says in 1 Timothy 4:12,

"Let no one look down on your youthfulness, but rather in speech, conduct, love, faith and purity, show yourself an example of those who believe."

God desires for us to shine as examples, especially to those whom we have influence over. The problem comes when we attempt to do this in our own strength. God wants us to live in love, purity, and faith, but to do this we first have to be saturated with Jesus' love.

Jesus says in John 15:12,

"This is My commandment, that you love one another, just as I have loved you."

We as Christians are called to love one another. Jesus gives us the key to doing this: we are able to love others because of His love for us. We do not have to be perfect in front of others, but we do need to continue believing that His finished work on the cross is enough. As His love encourages us to seek Him, He fills us with the Holy Spirit and gives us grace to move forward.

Loving others sometimes means laying aside our own agendas for the good of those around us. We can do this because the greatest hero of all lay down His life on a cross. Even though His divinity and perfection entitled Him to enjoy a long life, He still gave up everything for those He loved. He laid down all of His rights for us. Sometimes, when I think about being a man, I think about being a hero. When I think about being a hero, now I think about being more like Jesus.

- APPLICATION -

1. Do you ever feel conflicted between your agenda and God's agenda? Do you trust that He has good plans?

2. Can you think of any practical ways you could lay your life down for Christ today? I encourage you to listen to the Holy Spirit as you interact with others.

- FINAL THOUGHTS -

In the New Testament, Paul writes a lot about the flesh and its desires. He makes it clear that as we become more like Jesus, we need to continually sacrifice our flesh. That means we are laying down what we want in the natural sense and accepting what Jesus has for us. To do this, we must believe that He really does have good plans for us.

- DAY TWENTY-NINE -

Walking the Narrow Path

"To him the doorkeeper opens, and the sheep hear his voice, and he calls his own sheep by name and leads them out. When he puts forth all his own, he goes ahead of them, and the sheep follow him because they know his voice."

John 10:3-4

Have you ever found yourself wandering from the path that God has laid out for you? We start out glued to the narrow road, but there are temptations and trials along the way that can shift our direction away from God.

Jesus says in Matthew 7:14,

"For the gate is small and the way is narrow that leads to life, and there are few who find it."

We are told to take the narrow way, but how do we live in such a way that we remain on the narrow path? I am not talking about losing the salvation that Jesus has bought for us. I am referring to mistakes and distractions that cause our feet to slip, moving us out of His will in certain areas. Despite failures, God always gives us a way to step back onto the narrow path.

Let us take a look at someone very close to Jesus who let his feet begin to slip. Peter had traveled with Jesus every day for three years. He had followed Jesus and listened to His teaching, but nonetheless, Peter let his feet slip during the moment of truth. I want to look at one reason why this may have happened. More importantly, I want to examine the motivation behind his return to the narrow path.

Though it was a difficult road at times, following Jesus also had its perks. You see, Jesus' followers were under the impression that He was going to be their king—that He was going to restore the nation of Israel to freedom. On the night of His arrest, all those hopes went away. As soon as the perks were gone and the difficulties showed up, Peter ran away too. Now, we can be upset with Peter for deserting Jesus, but we must remember how many times we have run away from God's plans because we were scared of the plans of man.

On the morning of the resurrection, the report came that Jesus had risen. While some of the disciples refused to believe the testimony about Jesus, Peter got up and ran to the tomb:

> *"But these words appeared to them as nonsense, and they would not believe them. But Peter got up and ran to the tomb; stooping and looking in, he saw the linen wrappings only; and he went away to his home, marveling at what had happened."*
>
> Luke 24:11-12

Peter's feet had slipped. In a sense, he had strayed from the narrow path. He had walked in a direction that God had not intended, but the report about Jesus rising sent him running as fast as he could to see if it was true. I believe that he was starting to run back onto the narrow path—back into God's plan for his life. He was not running because he thought that all the extra incentives had come back. He was not running because the chance of being arrested had left. He was running because he thought that Jesus had come back.

When Jesus tells us to walk through the small gate, He is referring to Himself. When He says to walk the narrow path, He means for us to walk the path that He is walking. He wants us to walk beside Him. To continue on the narrow path, we must be abiding in Christ and allowing Him to live in us. Part of our journey as believers is to grow daily in our relationship with our Savior. Jesus lets us know how to do this in John 15:9:

> *"Just as the Father has loved Me, I have also loved you; abide in My love."*

Our relationship with Jesus should be motivated by the love He has shown us. He gave us life by being a sacrifice for us when we deserved death. I do not want to miss out on being friends with someone who willingly did that for me. Love is the greatest incentive, and we know that God's love for us never ends. Life's incentives leave, and fortune is lost. The amazing thing about walking with Jesus is that He will never leave us and He never gets lost.

- APPLICATION -

1. What are practical ways to abide in Christ?

2. Does your prayer time reflect a real relationship, or is it a repetition of Christian phrases? I want to encourage you to pray honestly before God. He desires you to grow in intimacy with Him because He loves knowing you.

- FINAL THOUGHTS -

Hearing the voice of God is important to having a strong relationship with Jesus. It was Jesus' personal words to Peter that restored him after his mistake. If you feel like you have trouble hearing from God on a personal level, ask God what He wants to say to you when you read the Bible. The Holy Spirit desires to speak directly to you. I encourage you to start by reading the words of Jesus in John 10:16 and John 10:27.

– DAY THIRTY –
Still Believing

"Great and marvelous are Your works, O Lord God, the Almighty; Righteous and true are Your ways, King of the nations! Who will not fear, O Lord, and glorify Your name? For You alone are holy; For all the nations will come and worship before You, For Your righteous acts have been revealed."

Revelation 15:3b-4

Have you ever felt like God has let you down? Have you ever felt like God was the only one who could have done something and He forgot to act? Though I have felt this way many times, I know that God is perfect and we are imperfect. God has better plans than us, but the feeling that God is at fault can still creep up on us. During these times, it is a good thing that God's grace is still sufficient.

In John chapter 11, Mary and Martha probably experience a feeling similar to the one I just described. After their brother, Lazarus, gets deathly sick, they send Jesus an appeal for help.

Verses 3b-4 say,

"'Lord, behold, he whom You love is sick.' But when Jesus heard this, He said, 'This sickness is not to end in death, but for the glory of God, so that the Son of God may be glorified by it.'"

Jesus states that the sickness is not going to be the end of Lazarus, but He chooses not to rush to the scene. Jesus hangs out for another couple of days before departing. Have you ever felt like God is hanging out when He should be acting on your behalf? Jesus is not just wasting time. Verse 4 shows us that His reason for waiting is determined by His desire to bring glory to God.

By the time Jesus arrives, He is too late and Lazarus is dead. It seems like Martha and Mary have a pretty good reason to be upset with Jesus. After all, He could have healed their brother if He had only acted sooner.

Verse 21 says,

"Martha then said to Jesus, 'Lord, if You had been here, my brother would not have died.'"

She bluntly reminds Jesus of His ability (or maybe even supposed responsibility) to do something. Have you ever said "You let this happen" to God? God knows and He still cares.

Now we get to the part of the story where Martha says something spectacular, and it is something that some of us say too infrequently.

In verse 22, she says,

"'Even now I know that whatever You ask of God, God will give You.'"

Martha is basically saying to Jesus, "I'm not happy with the way things have turned out. I'm hurt and disappointed, but even now... "Even now I know that whatever You ask of God, God will give You."

Martha understands that God is still in control, and that He can still do all things. The problem we often face is not God's sluggishness. The problem we face is that we have stopped believing what God has said because we do not like the state He let things get into.

Soon after this statement by Martha, Jesus raises Lazarus to life. He is God, after all. It is not too late. It is not too difficult for Him. It is still not too difficult for Him today.

Isaiah 55:8-9 says,

"'For My thoughts are not your thoughts, nor are your ways My ways,' declares the Lord. 'For as the heavens are higher than the earth, so are My ways higher than your ways and My thoughts than your thoughts.'"

We need to do what Martha did. We need to believe that God is still God, no matter the situation. He desires for us to believe He can still do all things and He still has a good plan in mind for us. The way we believe this is by continuously returning to the scene of the cross. Start with what you *do* believe. I believe that Jesus died on the cross so that I could have life—so that I could be made righteous before God. Someone who loves me enough to do that is Someone I can trust to have my best in mind. Because of His great love for me, I choose to walk in belief no matter what state my life is in. No matter what, His grace is there to pick us up. No matter what, His love and friendship will see us through.

- APPLICATION -

1. Do you feel like God has let you down in some way? Have you talked honestly with Him about it?

2. Is your trust in your situation or in God's love for you?

- FINAL THOUGHTS -

Perspective is vital in life. If we believe that our own plans are the most important thing, then we are going to get discouraged. We need to accept a higher perspective. This earth is passing away, but God's Word is eternal. Better still, His love for us never ends.

- THANK YOU -

Thank you for joining me these last 30 days. If you have enjoyed this devotional book, please consider giving me your feedback by writing a review of *30 Days of Inspiration and Hope* on Amazon.com or GoodReads.com. I appreciate your comments.

It takes a lot of time and effort to put together the books I publish and the videos I create. You can help support me by purchasing a copy of this book for a friend, loved one, or someone who may benefit from reading it.

You can also show your support by purchasing a copy of my testimony story, *My Mess*. Another simple way to support me is by sharing the videos I post online. Finally, you can also book me to speak at your service or Christian event. I thank you for every bit of support that I receive and I pray that God has been able to bless you through this book.

In Christ,
Troy Black

- THE AUTHOR -

Troy Black lives with his wife, Leslie, in East Texas. He likes board games, playing sports, reading, and going for long walks. Troy and Leslie have three daughters named Mirabelle, Iona, and Lauralee.

Troy and his wife started Inspire Christian Books out of a passion to spread the Gospel and the Truth of God's Word. It is their desire to see those who are lost come to salvation in Christ Jesus and for the Christian church to experience abundant life through the work of the Holy Spirit.

- CONTACT US -

TroyBlackVideos.com | *InspireChristianBooks.com*

Printed in Great Britain
by Amazon